FATTY LIVER DIET COOKBOOK

THE ULTIMATE GUIDE WITH 150+ RECIPES FOR YOUR HEALTH

RITA DUNCAN

© **Copyright 2022 - All rights reserved**.

This document is geared towards providing exact and reliable information in regard to the topic and issue covered.

- From a Declaration of Principles which was accepted and approved equally by a Committee of the American Bar Association and a Committee of Publishers and Associations.

In no way is it legal to reproduce, duplicate, or transmit any part of this document in either electronic means or in printed format. All rights reserved.

The information provided herein is stated to be truthful and consistent, in that any liability, in terms of inattention or otherwise, by any usage or abuse of any policies, processes, or directions contained within is the solitary and utter responsibility of the recipient reader. Under no circumstances will any legal responsibility or blame be held against the publisher for any reparation, damages, or monetary loss due to the information herein, either directly or indirectly.

Respective authors own all copyrights not held by the publisher.

The information herein is offered for informational purposes solely and is universal as so. The presentation of the information is without contract or any type of guarantee assurance.

The trademarks that are used are without any consent, and the publication of the trademark is without permission or backing by the trademark owner. All trademarks and brands within this book are for clarifying purposes only and are owned by the owners themselves, not affiliated with this document.

Table of Contents

TABLE OF CONTENTS 3

INTRODUCTION 7

CHAPTER 1. WHAT IS MEANT BY A FATTY LIVER 8

    TYPE OF FATTY LIVER? 8
        Alcohol-Related Fatty Liver Disease (ALD) 8
        Non-Alcohol Related Fatty Liver Disease (NAFLD) 9
    WHAT CAUSES NAFLD? 9
        Nutritional Deficiencies 9
        Obesity, Type 2 Diabetes, and Insulin Resistance 9
    WHAT ARE THE 4 STAGES OF CIRRHOSIS OF THE LIVER? 10
        Stage One: Inflammation 10
        Stage Two: Scarring or Fibrosis 10
        Stage Three: Cirrhosis 10
        Stage Four: ESLD (End-Stage Liver Disease) 10

CHAPTER 2. DIAGNOSIS AND TREATMENTS REGARDING FATTY LIVER 11

    DIAGNOSIS 11
        The "At Home Test" 11
        A Physical Exam 11
        Blood Tests 11
        Imaging 11
    TREATMENTS 12
    DIET GUIDE FOR CIRRHOSIS AND ADVANCED LIVER DISEASES 13
        Compensated Cirrhosis 13
        Decompensated Cirrhosis 14
        Fluid Retention 14

CHAPTER 3. THE FUNDAMENTAL ROLE THAT FASTING AND EXCERCISE CAN PLAY 15

    IMPORTANCE OF FASTING 15
        Intermittent Fasting 15

        Benefits of Intermittent Fasting 15
        How to Follow an Intermittent Fasting Schedule 16
    IMPORTANCE OF PHYSICAL ACTIVITY 16
        High-Intensity Interval Training (HIIT) 16
        Benefits of HITT 17
        Simple HIIT Workouts You Can Do Anywhere 18
        Will HIIT Heal a Fatty Liver? 18

CHAPTER 4. THE IMPORTANCE OF FOLLOWING A WELL-DEFINED DIET 20

    DIETARY APPROACHES TO TREATING A FATTY LIVER 20
    DIET GUIDE FOR VARIOUS FATTY LIVER CONDITIONS 20
        Alcoholic Liver Disease (ALD) 20
        Non Alcoholic Fatty Liver Disease (NAFLD) 21
        Acute Viral Hepatitis 21
        Chronic Viral Hepatitis 21
        Autoimmune Hepatitis 22
        Haemochromatosis 22
        Wilson's Disease 22
        Gilbert's Syndrome 23

CHAPTER 5. FOODS SUITABLE FOR THE FATTY LIVER DIET 24

    FOODS TO ENJOY 24
    FOODS TO LIMIT 25
    FOODS TO BE AVOIDED 25

CHAPTER 6. IMPORTANCE OF HAVING A HEALTHY LIVER 26

    DIGESTION AND METABOLISM 26
    DETOXIFICATION 26
    IMMUNITY 27
    STORAGE 27
    OTHER IMPORTANT FUNCTIONS OF THE LIVER 27
    CAUSES OF FATTY LIVER 27
    SYMPTOMS 28
    PROBLEMS 28

    Common Comorbidities 29

CHAPTER 7. COMPLICATIONS WHEN NAFLD IS IGNORED 30

    NASH 30

    FIBROSIS 30

    CIRRHOSIS 30

    LIVER CANCER 31

    LIVER FAILURE 31

    PREVENTION OF FATTY LIVER DISEASE 31

CHAPTER 8. DRINK AND SMOOTHIE RECIPES 32

    1. LETTUCE, BANANA, AND BERRIES SMOOTHIE 32

    2. APPLE, QUINOA, AND FIG SMOOTHIE 32

    3. STRAWBERRY SHAKE 32

    4. SWEET SUNRISE SMOOTHIE 33

    5. GREEN SEA MOSS DRINK 33

    6. BANANA HERBAL DRINK 33

    7. WATERMELON, CANTALOUPE, AND MANGO SMOOTHIE 34

    8. BLACKBERRY AND BANANA SMOOTHIE 34

    9. GREEN SMOOTHIE WITH RASPBERRIES 35

    10. VEGGIE-FUL SMOOTHIE 35

    11. APPLE PIE SMOOTHIE 35

    12. ORANGE AND LETTUCE SMOOTHIE 36

    13. GREEN TEA AND LETTUCE DETOX SMOOTHIE 36

    14. CHAMOMILE DELIGHT SMOOTHIE 36

    15. HONEY DEW AND ARUGULA SMOOTHIE 37

    16. WATERMELON AND STRAWBERRIES DRINK 37

    17. SWEET GREEN DRINK 37

    18. BANANA SEA MOSS SMOOTHIE 38

    19. SMOOTHIE BOWL 38

    20. REFRESHING SMOOTHIE WITH NUTS 38

    21. CANTALOUPE SMOOTHIE TEA 39

    22. WATERMELON JUICE 39

    23. GREEN SMOOTHIE 40

CHAPTER 9. BREAKFAST RECIPES 41

    24. LIVER DETOX SMOOTHIE 41

    25. HIGH PROTEIN FRENCH TOAST 41

    26. BROCCOLI SALAD 41

    27. CLASSIC EGGS BENEDICT WITH LEMON BASIL HOLLANDAISE .42

    28. BLUEBERRY SMOOTHIE 42

    29. FRIED EGG AND GREENS 43

    30. SWEET POTATO PIE SMOOTHIE BOWL 43

    31. CORNMEAL PANCAKES WITH BLACK BEAN SALSA AND CILANTRO YOGURT 43

    32. SOUTHWESTERN-STYLE BLACK BEAN BURRITOS .. 44

    33. FRUIT YOGURT PARFAIT 45

    34. PEANUT BUTTER MAPLE BANANA MUFFINS 45

    35. ULTIMATE LIVER DETOX SOUP 46

    36. PINEAPPLE, MATCHA, AND BEET CHIA PUDDING . 46

    37. CHICKEN SOUVLAKI 47

    38. OVERNIGHT SUPERFOOD PARFAIT 47

    39. ONION OMELET 48

    40. STUFFED FIGS 48

    41. SUPERFOOD LIVER CLEANSING SOUP 48

    42. ASPARAGUS WITH EGG 49

    43. VANILLA OATS 49

    44. CARROT OMELET 50

    45. VEGGIE OMELET 50

    46. BEETS OMELET 50

    47. SPICED FRENCH TOAST 51

CHAPTER 10. LUNCH RECIPES 52

    48. MIXED VEGGIES AND GRAPEFRUIT SALAD WITH DIJON GRAPEFRUIT VINAIGRETTE 52

    49. QUICK HUMMUS AND GREEK SALAD 52

    50. QUICK PESTO CHICKEN SALAD WITH GREENS 53

    51. CRISPY TOFU WITH VEGETABLE SALAD 53

    52. HEALTHY SPINACH SALAD 54

    53. ROASTED CHICKEN AND MUSHROOMS SALAD 55

    54. CHICKPEA, BROCCOLI, AND POMEGRANATE SALAD 55

    55. ANCHOVY, ORANGE, AND OLIVE SALAD 56

    56. VEGETABLE AND CHICKPEA SALAD 56

    57. TABOULI WITH VEGGIES SALAD 57

    58. HEALTHY FATTOUSH SALAD 58

    59. VEGGIES WITH CHICKPEA SALAD 58

    60. CHEESY SCRAMBLED EGGS WITH FRESH HERBS . 59

61. Couscous With Artichokes, Sun-Dried Tomatoes, and Feta 59
62. Lemon Muffins 60
63. Citrus Chicken With Delicious Cold Soup 60
64. Eggs and Veggies 61
65. Toxin Flush and Detox Salad............................ 61
66. Olive and Milk Bread 62

CHAPTER 11. POULTRY AND MEAT 63

67. Chicken and Lemongrass Sauce 63
68. Sesame Chicken With Black Rice, Broccoli, and Snap Peas 63
69. Tasty Lamb Ribs 64
70. Saffron Beef 64
71. Chicken and Butter Sauce 64
72. Lemon and Garlic Barbecued Ocean Trout With Green Salad.. 65
73. Chicken and Black Beans 65
74. Sweet Chipotle Grilled Beef Ribs 66
75. Grilled Sirloin Steak With Sauce Diane 66
77. Rib Roast With Roasted Shallots and Garlic 67
78. Beef Meatballs 68
79. Pot Roast 68
80. Beef Tripe Pot 68
81. Beef Stovies 69
82. Festive Turkey Rouladen 69
83. Pan-Fried Chorizo Sausage 70
84. Chinese Bok Choy and Turkey Soup 70
85. Herby Chicken Meatloaf 71
86. Lovely Pulled Chicken Egg Bites 71

CHAPTER 12. FISH AND SEAFOOD 72

87. Shrimp With Garlic.. 72
88. Sabich Sandwich 72
89. Salmon With Vegetables.................................. 73
90. Crispy Fish... 73
91. Moules Marinieres 74
92. Steamed Mussels With Coconut-Curry 74
93. Tuna Noodle Casserole 74
94. Salmon Burgers... 75
95. Seared Scallops... 75
96. Black COD 76
97. Miso-Glazed Salmon 76
98. Arugula and Sweet Potato Salad............................. 76
99. Nicoise Salad 77
100. Shrimp Curry 77
101. Salmon Pasta 78
102. Crab Legs 78
103. Crusty Pesto Salmon 78
104. Buttery Cod 79
105. Sesame Tuna Steak 79
106. Lemon Garlic Shrimp 79
107. Foil Packet Salmon 80

CHAPTER 13. VEGETABLES 81

108. Parsley Zucchini and Radishes 81
109. Cherry Tomatoes Sauté 81
110. Creamy Eggplant 81
111. Eggplant and Carrots Mix 82
112. Parmesan Eggplants 82
113. Kale Sauté..82
114. Carrots Sauté 83
115. Bok Choy and Sprouts 83
116. Balsamic Radishes 83
117. Spaghetti Squash Casserole 84
118. Cinnamon Baby Carrot 84
119. Eggplant Tongues 85
120. Super Tasty Onion Petals 85
121. Eggplant Garlic Salad With Tomatoes 85
122. Curry Eggplants 86
123. Sauteed Asparagus 86
124. Roasted Apple With Bacon 86
125. Fennel Slices 87
126. Butternut Squash Rice..87
127. Eggplant Lasagna 88
128. Stuffed Eggplants With Cherry Tomatoes.............88

CHAPTER 14. SALADS 89

129. Satisfying Spring Salad 89
130. The Raw Green Detox Salad 89
131. Dandelion Salad 90
132. Spicy Wakame Salad 90
133. Avo-Orange Salad Dish 91
134. Nourishing Electric Salad 91
135. Superfood Fonio Salad 91
136. Healthy Chickpea Roast Salad 92
137. Amaranth Tabbouleh Salad 92
138. Zucchini and Mushroom Bowl 93
139. Pear and Strawberry Salad 93
140. Raspberry and Arugula Salad 93
141. Mixed Berries Salad 94
142. Apple and Kale Salad 94
143. Mango and Arugula Salad 94
144. Orange and Kale Salad 95
145. Zucchini and Tomato Salad 95
146. Tomato and Arugula Salad 95
147. Warm Avo and Quinoa Salad 96
148. Chickpeas and Quinoa Salad 96
149. Quinoa, Tomato, and Mango Salad 97

CHAPTER 15. SNACKS 98

150. Falafel 98
151. Sloppy Joe 98
152. Sausage Links 99
153. Chickpea Nuggets 99

CHAPTER 16. 28-DAY MEAL PLAN 100

CONCLUSION 102

INDEX 103

Introduction

Dead liver cells are responsible for the buildup of fat in the body and help create a fatty liver. Over time, excess weight can add up to cause an actual fat-filled disease in some people known as non-alcoholic fatty liver disease. Obese people have more than four times the risk of this condition than those who are slender and one-third of obese people with NAFLD may develop cirrhosis, which causes damage to the underlying structure of organs. This syndrome is often associated with obesity, but it's not always tied to being overweight or eating unhealthy food. In fact, it develops from excessive alcohol consumption or high blood pressure complications from pregnancy and birth. Patients with NAFLD are at a high and increased risk of developing cirrhosis. In fact, it's been found that 15 percent of Americans may have this condition. Fatty liver disease can also lead to serious complications in some people, including those with diabetes and heart disease. Diabetic patients have nearly double the risk of developing fatty liver. It's also known that pregnant women who drink alcohol (in moderation) may protect their children with high-fat diets, but it can be harmful to their own fetuses during development. Women who are suffering from high blood pressure may be more likely to develop these complications from the fatty liver as well. Increased alcohol consumption can cause a buildup of fat in the liver. High-fat diets that are rich in calories and poor in nutrition also increase their risks of fatty liver. Being obese increases their risk, as well, but it's not the only factor involved. Fat deposits are stored more easily in people who have insulin resistance and diabetes mellitus. This is known as metabolic syndrome, which is also responsible for high blood pressure and high cholesterol, and triglyceride levels.

The best way to prevent fatty liver disease is by making lifestyle changes that reduce the risk factors for this condition. If you're pregnant, increase your exercise and maintain a healthy diet. Don't drink alcohol when you have diabetes or are on a high-fat diet. Prevent high blood pressure and keep your weight down.

Treatment of fatty liver disease is difficult in many cases. The patient's symptoms of NAFLD can include fatigue, anorexia, swollen legs, and belly pain that develops in the morning before it's felt elsewhere. However, liver damage may be worse than expected, which can lead to breathing problems, coma, and death if left untreated. It's important to work with your doctor to achieve successful treatment of the condition through diet plans, medication if necessary, and exercises. Exercise improves circulation throughout the body by increasing blood flow. This helps eliminate fat in the liver and it also reduces high blood sugar. To avoid developing these conditions, lose weight if you're obese. If you have diabetes or metabolic syndrome, control your blood sugar intake through diet and medication if necessary to prevent complications of fatty liver disease. Eat healthy foods low in saturated fat, trans fats, and cholesterol such as fruits, vegetables, whole grains, and lean meats. Work with your doctor for a safe exercise program that's right for you.

When you have finished reading this book, I invite you to leave a review. This would mean so much to me as it would help the dissemination of this material. I really worked hard on this product, I really hope you enjoy it!

Chapter 1. What Is Meant by a Fatty Liver

Fatty liver literally means that you have excess fat in your liver. You may have also heard it referred to as hepatic steatosis. Put simply, it occurs when the liver cells, known as hepatocytes, become so filled with fat that it affects their ability, and therefore the liver's ability, to function effectively. Your liver is like a factory that never sleeps. The liver is divided into three functioning parts: the processing plant, the distribution center, and the storehouse. As your liver processes the blood that it receives from the body, it breaks down the nutrients from your food and distributes these vital nutrients back to the rest of your body so it can better absorb them. These nutrients help to make the blood plasma proteins and other key elements that are helpful in aiding digestion. The liver will hold on to any extra nutrients that you do not need to use right away and store them safely for future use. It also processes any toxins entering your body through your food and is able to eliminate them before they can harm you.

When your liver is functioning efficiently, it is the major fat-burning organ in your body and is able to pump excessive fat within your body out through the bile and excrete it as feces. While a healthy liver will help keep your weight under control, an unhealthy liver will cause fat to build up in your liver and in the rest of your body. Your liver itself will become swollen and full of toxic fat. This begins to block the pathways that blood normally flows along and makes it difficult for the blood to be cleansed properly. When this happens, the blood that is returning to the heart is full of unhealthy fats and toxins and can damage your heart, and immune system as well. When your liver becomes overwhelmed with too many toxins and fatty cells over time, it ceases to be able to do its job. It cannot function properly and this causes a backup in the liver. It also means that your blood will not circulate properly, important nutrients cannot be delivered to other vital organs, and your body cannot detoxify naturally, so even more toxins will build up in your liver. This vicious cycle is the result of fatty liver disease and it needs to be addressed by crucial lifestyle changes to prevent even more serious, and potentially fatal, health complications from arising.

Type of Fatty Liver?

There are two various types of fatty liver disease: Alcohol-Related Fatty Liver Disease (ALD) and Non-Alcohol Related Fatty Liver Disease (NAFLD).

Alcohol-Related Fatty Liver Disease (ALD)

Alcohol-related liver disease is caused by the heavy consumption of alcohol. The liver breaks down alcohol, therefore, the more alcohol you consume, the more the liver needs to process, and the more damage is caused. The good news is that fatty liver disease related to alcohol consumption is preventable. And if you do have it, it can improve once you stop drinking.

If you do not stop drinking, however, serious complications can arise. Some of these complications include an enlarged liver, which can cause pain and discomfort; alcoholic hepatitis, which is swelling in the liver and can cause jaundice, nausea, vomiting, fevers, and pain; and alcoholic cirrhosis, which is a buildup of scar tissue in your liver and can lead to liver failure if left untreated.

In addition to the above complications, about 30% of people with alcohol-induced liver disease have the hepatitis C virus and about 50% of them develop gallstones as well. People with alcohol-induced liver disease are also at greater risk of cancer of the liver, kidney problems, intestinal bleeding, fluid in the belly, confusion, and severe infections.

While we focused on the healing of non-alcohol-related complications with the liver, it is important to address how to repair alcohol-related liver damage as well. The goal of treatment is to restore normal function to the liver. The first step to making this happen is actually fairly simple. You must stop drinking alcohol completely. Oftentimes, this may involve treatment programs to help guide and support you. Dietary changes can also be very helpful for alcohol-related liver damage. If you believe that you have liver damage related to alcohol consumption, make sure to follow the plan that is laid out to put yourself on the pathway to healing. If the liver damage is severe enough, more serious treatment measures may be necessary. But no improvements or healing can begin unless an alcohol detox occurs first.

Non-Alcohol Related Fatty Liver Disease (NAFLD)

NAFLD, or non-alcohol-related fatty liver disease, is the term used to describe the buildup of extra fat in the liver in individuals who use little or no alcohol. As the fat builds up in the liver cells, liver inflammation sets up, which can cause varying degrees of scarring and damage. In the United States, NAFLD may impact up to one in three to one in five adults and about one in ten children, making it a fairly prevalent condition.

When NAFLD is left untreated it can lead to more serious conditions such as Non-Alcoholic Steatohepatitis (NASH). NASH is a serious condition that causes severe scarring of the liver and cirrhosis. Cirrhosis occurs when the liver cells are gradually replaced by scar tissue because of the damage done by inflammation and fat accumulation. It is not uncommon to need a liver transplant once advanced cirrhosis occurs. The scar tissue impairs the liver's ability to function properly and repair itself.

What Causes NAFLD?

Nutritional Deficiencies

Nutrition plays a huge impact on the health of the liver. Those whose diets are high in refined carbohydrates and unhealthy fats, and low in antioxidant and plant foods, are at a much higher risk of NAFLD. Their dietary choices put them at risk of vitamin C, vitamin D, vitamin E, and selenium deficiencies, which are all necessary for liver health. Addressing these deficiencies and incorporating the proper sources of nutrition and micronutrients goes a long way to repairing liver damage and will be laid out in detail in later chapters.

Obesity, Type 2 Diabetes, and Insulin Resistance

One of the most common conditions thought to be a cause of fatty infiltration of the liver is obesity. It is believed that two-thirds of obese adults and half of obese children may, in fact, have a fatty liver. About 20% of those who are obese may suffer from the more severe condition NASH. But, in reality, it is not obesity that causes NAFLD as much as NAFLD occurs as you are becoming obese.

The presence of type 2 diabetes and other metabolic conditions associated with obesity, including insulin resistance, are known risk factors for the development of a fatty liver.

Insulin is a hormone secreted by the pancreas and its main function is to regulate the number of nutrients, particularly glucose, fats, and proteins, circulating in your bloodstream. While insulin is usually recognized for its role in blood sugar management, it also greatly affects fat and protein metabolism as well.

Fat cells can only hold a certain amount of fat. When maximum capacity is reached, insulin will keep trying to put fat into the cells but they will refuse to accept it. While your pancreas continues to release insulin to attempt to lower blood sugar levels, your cells stop responding to this signal. This results in a rise in both blood sugar and insulin levels in your blood. This increase in production by the pancreas begins to tax this organ over time and it will eventually lead to a decreased amount of insulin being produced. When this occurs, your blood sugar will begin to exceed the safe threshold level and this causes type 2 diabetes.

One of the main factors that can contribute to insulin resistance is believed to be an increased level of carbohydrates in your diet. When you eat a meal containing a large amount of refined carbohydrates, the amount of sugar in your bloodstream increases. This signals the pancreas to release insulin into your blood, which then signals your cells to pick up the sugar from your blood in order to reduce blood sugar levels. When cells stop responding to insulin correctly and are unable to absorb any more glucose from the blood, insulin resistance occurs.

When the cells are unable to hold any more fat, the excess fat ends up being stored around all of your internal organs, including your liver cells. Once this occurs, you officially have a fatty liver.

What Are the 4 Stages of Cirrhosis of the Liver?

Liver Cirrhosis occurs in stages. Namely:

Stage One: Inflammation

The first sign of liver disease is inflammation which causes it to be slightly enlarged and tender. Inflammation is usually a sign that your body is employing its natural defense tactics to fight an infection, heal an injury, or any foreign intrusion in order to restore health.

However, if inflammation keeps getting triggered by what is attacking your liver the damage becomes more than the benefit and can actually result in serious damage to your liver. The tricky thing about liver inflammation is that unlike most other inflammations that will give you a sign that there is inflammation through redness, pain, or elevated temperature; it does not give any form of discomfort and therefore it becomes very difficult to identify liver inflammation. If, however, your doctor is able to identify inflammation in your liver during a routine checkup, it becomes very easy to stop the problem that could be causing this in its tracks before it progresses and causes serious damage to your liver. It is therefore important to schedule routine checkups.

Stage Two: Scarring or Fibrosis

When inflammation is not identified, it leads to scarring that's literally formed every time the inflammation goes down only to come back again and again, considering how tender the liver is. This scarring when uncontrolled continues growing to the point that it now replaces what used to be your healthy liver tissue. The bad thing about this is the fact that scarred tissue cannot do the same work that your previously healthy liver tissue could. As more and more fibrosis occurs, your liver tissue starts losing sensitivity and its functions start getting impaired as it has to work many times harder than it should to get a simple function done. If you are able to get an accurate diagnosis at this stage, your doctor will prescribe medication and a lifestyle change that will restore your liver to health in a relatively short duration.

Stage Three: Cirrhosis

Cirrhosis is a condition in which the entire liver has developed scar tissue, replacing the soft liver tissue with hard scar tissue. The liver will struggle and work hard to do its duties, but if the condition is not treated, it will fail and be unable to work at all or, in the worst case, ineffectively.

This is the point when the symptoms become apparent. It's critical that you get medical attention right away if you begin to exhibit the earlier listed symptoms. Your doctor will immediately focus on treating the condition to stop it from spreading after they have made the correct diagnosis. Once this has been accomplished, attention will turn to restoration, which will be a purposefully gradual process to prevent the harm from getting worse.

Stage Four: ESLD (End-Stage Liver Disease)

At this stage, your liver is fully done in and there is very little chance of reversal as decompensation has occurred and the only option is a liver transplant. Decompensation usually includes an impairment of your kidney function, encephalopathy, lung problems, variceal bleeding, and fluid retention in your abdomen that has to be physically drained. For this reason, such a patient is given priority on the liver transplant list.

Chapter 2. Diagnosis and Treatments Regarding Fatty Liver

Diagnosis

There are several tests used to diagnose liver damage and fatty liver disease, either intentionally or unintentionally.

The "At Home Test"

I would describe this test as a screening to see if it is likely that you have a fatty liver rather than an actual test, but it is very useful as an indicator. You will need a tape measure for this screening. While standing, take three slow deep breaths and exhale fully. At the end of the third breath, while relaxed, measure the circumference of your waist at a point in between your belly button and your pelvic (hip) bones on your sides. This measurement should be less than half of your height. If it is more than half of your height, there is a very good chance that you have a fatty liver.

A Physical Exam

Hepatomegaly, or abnormal enlargement of the liver, is one of the very few physical indications that you may have NAFLD. When the liver is larger than normal, this points to fatty accumulation and inflammation. This can be more difficult to assess in overweight or obese individuals where it is easily missed, so it is not a reliable form of detection.

It is possible that during a surgical procedure that is unrelated to a liver assessment, the doctor may recognize that your liver appears larger, more discolored, or differently textured than is deemed normal. All of these are also indicators of liver disease and should prompt immediate further testing and investigation.

There are not many obvious physical abnormalities that are easily detected during a physical exam, therefore, this is not a primary source of diagnosis for a fatty liver.

Blood Tests

A blood test can assess how well the liver is functioning. One of the most common blood tests determines the level of certain liver enzymes (proteins) present in the blood. In a healthy, functioning liver, the enzymes should mostly be contained within the cells of the liver so that the level of enzymes in the blood remains relatively low. However, if the liver is not working properly, these enzymes will spill over into the bloodstream. The enzymes that are the best indicator of how well the liver is functioning are the aminotransferases. These include aspartate aminotransferase (AST) and alanine aminotransferase (ALT). When either of these numbers is elevated, it is a good indication that liver disease is occurring. These numbers can help the doctor assess the level of inflammation and damage, and additional blood tests might be ordered to find out if you have other health conditions that are increasing your liver enzyme levels.

Imaging

Routine imaging tests can show fatty deposits in your liver. There are several common types of imaging.

Ultrasound

An ultrasound creates an image of the anatomy of your organs by using a device called a transducer to bounce sound waves off of them. It is used to examine the liver's size, shape, texture, and blood supply. The presence of fatty deposits in the liver is indicated if the liver appears extremely bright in an ultrasound imaging. The liver tissue may also seem brilliant due to cirrhosis.

Computed Tomography (CT)

A CT scan uses a combination of both x-rays and computer technology to create an image of your liver. If the liver appears to have a lower density than other organs, this most likely indicates the presence of a fatty liver.

Magnetic Resonance Imaging (MRI)

An MRI scan makes use of radio waves and magnets, without using x-rays, to produce a detailed image of the organs and surrounding soft tissues. This type of imaging has the greatest sensitivity for diagnosing NAFLD but does not do a good job of distinguishing the level of severity of the fatty liver.

Elastography

Elastography is a newer form of imaging that can help diagnose more advanced stages of liver disease, such as liver fibrosis. Some different types of elastography include vibration-controlled transient elastography (which is a special type of ultrasound); shear wave elastography (a different form of ultrasound that determines liver stiffness); and magnetic resonance elastography (a special type of MRI to measure liver stiffness).

Liver Biopsy

A liver biopsy is really one of the only true means of detecting fatty liver disease. It involves taking a sample of the liver tissue through a fairly simple surgical procedure that involves ultrasound imaging and a needle. The sample can then be examined thoroughly under a microscope to identify if there are any signs of fatty liver disease, infection, inflammation, cancer, or scarring.

Treatments

Although there is no full cure for cirrhosis of the liver, there are treatments and management procedures that help in delaying its progress and reducing its symptoms and in so doing reduce the complications that come with liver disease and also reduce the damage done to the liver cells.

- Fluid retention in joints and the abdomen is first managed by following a very low-sodium diet. For extreme cases of ascites, the doctor may have to drain the fluid from your stomach. Diuretics may also be prescribed to help reduce the fluid buildup.
- If a patient's cirrhosis is a result of excessive alcohol consumption, then the first step is to refrain from any alcohol intake. This gives the liver a chance to take a break from the detoxification of toxins brought about by alcohol.
- A healthy, low-sodium, and balanced diet with recommended drug therapy can be used to help improve the disorientation and confused mental conditions of patients. In some cases, laxatives may be prescribed to help absorb toxins thus reducing the liver's job.
- A lifestyle change that includes a healthy and natural low-sodium diet and regular physical activity is recommended to all patients as it helps the body heal itself by tapping into its primal self-healing ability.
- For cirrhosis that was exacerbated by underlying medical conditions such as autoimmune diseases, the doctor will start by addressing the underlying conditions and in cases where the damage was not too much, the damage can actually be reversed.
- Patients with severe cirrhosis may need to get a liver transplant when all forms of treatment do not respond, and the damage to the liver continues to worsen.
- In cases of autoimmune hepatitis, the patient will be prescribed drugs that suppress the immune system such as azathioprine.

- For hemochromatosis patients, treatment will involve removing blood in order lower iron levels thus preventing further liver damage. In cases of Wilson's disease where there is excess copper in the blood and liver, drugs will be administered to increase the removal of copper from the body through the urine.
- Do not use non-steroidal anti-inflammatory medication. These include naproxen and ibuprofen. This is because patients with cirrhosis of the liver can further damage their livers and kidneys with such drugs.
- Individualized treatment of patients with hepatitis C. the reason for this is that not all patients are in a position to receive antiviral treatment as it could lead to further liver damage for some people. A doctor specializing in liver disease will carry out a series of tests to determine the best course of treatment.
- Vaccinating patients with cirrhosis against hepatitis A and B infections. This helps prevent further damage to the liver.

Diet Guide for Cirrhosis and Advanced Liver Diseases

Cirrhosis is a condition that makes your liver stop working properly and also affects its ability to release glycogen, a chemical that is required to provide energy to your body when you need it. When the liver is not able to release glycogen, your body starts using its own muscle tissues to provide energy. A situation like this can lead to conditions like malnutrition, weakness, and muscle wasting.

If your condition worsens and progresses to cirrhosis, you need to be very careful with your diet. You would need a diet that supports your liver function and also can save you from malnutrition. The best way is to immediately approach a certified doctor or dietician for a strategically designed diet plan.

Let's now talk about various types of cirrhosis conditions and what diet one should eat to keep the liver functioning.

Compensated Cirrhosis

Compensated cirrhosis is a condition where the liver is scarred severely but there are still enough healthy liver cells to perform all of its functions adequately. Even if you suffer from compensated cirrhosis, you may feel quite well due to the fact that the liver is still able to function the way it is supposed to.

In this condition, it is highly recommended to eat a well-balanced diet to make sure that your body is able to get adequate amounts of carbohydrates, protein, fat, vitamins, and minerals. It has been found in the studies that people suffering from cirrhosis, need more energy and proteins than a healthy person of the same weight.

You must ensure that you take protein and starch food with every meal, especially breakfast and evening meals. You should eat 25–35 kcal and 1–1.2 g of protein for every kg of your body weight per day. People who are underweight need to increase their energy and protein intake further.

Snacking between meals can top up your calories and protein. Try to eat regularly, say every two to three hours. The best choices of suitable snacks include:

- Teacake
- Toast
- Crackers
- Cereal
- Fruit
- Milky drinks

People suffering from cirrhosis may develop another condition called bone thinning or osteopenia /osteoporosis, which if not diagnosed on time may lead to bone fractures. This condition can be found only if diagnosed by bone density scanning called a DXA scan. If you do suffer from bone thinning, your doctor is more likely to prescribe you a vitamin D and/or calcium supplement.

Decompensated Cirrhosis

The second stage of cirrhosis and a dangerous one is called decompensated cirrhosis. This is a condition where the liver is not able to perform all of its normal functions. As a result, the patient may suffer from other severe conditions like fluid retention and mental confusion, known as encephalopathy.

For people suffering from decompensated cirrhosis, high-energy, and high-protein diet is recommended. To be more precise, you would need 35–40 kcal and 1.5 g of protein for every kg of your body weight per day. It is highly recommended that you must consult your certified doctor for further diet recommendations and treatment.

Fluid Retention

It has been found in the studies that some people, who have cirrhosis, may get a buildup of fluid in the stomach area. Other symptoms of this condition are swelling of the legs and feet. Due to the buildup of fluid in the stomach, one may feel bloated most of the time but it is highly recommended that the person should drink enough fluids to avoid dehydration.

Cutting down on the amount of common salt in your food can help control fluid retention. The recommendation is to keep the salt content balanced, not too high and not too low. The anticipated amount of salt or sodium reduction in your diet is approx. 5.2 g of salt per day.

The amount of salt in your own prepared food can be controlled but you may not control the salt contents in the foods that are available in the market. It is recommended that you always look at the labels on the food you buy. It will help you keep your salt intake in control.

The best place to look for this information is the nutrition information on the food label. You need to look for the amount of salt per 100 g. Food can be called low in salt if the salt content is up to 0.3 g salt or less per 100 g or 0.1 g sodium.

To receive your FREE eBook "The Anti-Inflammatory Cookbook" Scan this QR Code

Chapter 3. The Fundamental Role That Fasting and Excercise Can Play

Importance of Fasting

Intermittent Fasting

The term "intermittent fasting" (often referred to as "IF") refers to an eating pattern that includes voluntary fasting rather than a specific diet. It entails alternating periods of fasting and eating; it doesn't limit the kinds of things you can eat, but rather offers a schedule for when you should.

You will only eat at a certain time of day if you are intermittent fasting. Your body can burn fat if you fast for a set period of time each day. It functions by giving your body more time to burn off the calories from your most recent meal and by making your body start burning fat.

Incorporating intermittent fasting into your eating routine allows your body to detoxify more efficiently. It also helps you to better understand feelings of hunger. Fasting causes a metabolic shift that helps the body to more effectively regenerate, eliminate waste, and repair cells.

During your fasting periods, you are only allowed to consume water and beverages with no calories, such as tea or black coffee. During your eating periods, you should consume foods and meals that are recommended. Fasting in this way will allow you to better understand feelings of hunger.

Benefits of Intermittent Fasting

Weight Loss

Intermittent fasting promotes weight loss; particularly weight loss around the belly. This is especially important when you have a fatty liver because fat tends to accumulate in the belly region. Reducing and removing this fat is crucial when you are trying to repair liver damage.

Improved Blood Sugar Levels and Insulin Resistance

Intermittent fasting has been shown to counter insulin resistance; therefore, it can also help to reduce blood sugar levels and avoid or reverse the effects of type 2 diabetes. Insulin resistance, high blood sugar levels, and type 2 diabetes are all known risk factors that contribute to the building of fatty liver disease; combating these metabolic conditions is key to repairing liver damage.

Oxidative Stress

Oxidative stress is when free radicals in the body damage healthy cells and waste products to build up. Intermittent fasting can help to prevent oxidative stress by reducing inflammation in the cells, suppressing cell growth to prevent the formation of certain cancers, and protecting the cells from DNA damage.

Gut Healing

Intermittent fasting can help to increase the number of good bacteria in the gut and decrease the number of bad bacteria. Fasting gives your digestive system a period of rest. During this time, your gut is able to heal and this helps to prevent a "leaky gut" which can lead to other conditions such as Crohn's disease and Irritable Bowel Syndrome.

How to Follow an Intermittent Fasting Schedule

There are various different intermittent fasting methods, but they are all based on choosing regular time periods to eat and fast. I will describe four of the different intermittent fasting schedules you can follow. Each method has its own benefits. Pick the method that you feel would be the easiest for you to follow and will best suit your schedule and routine. It is also vital to speak with your doctor to make sure that intermittent fasting is safe for you to do.

12– 12 Fast

A twelve-hour fast simply means that you should eat for twelve hours during the day and then fast for the remaining twelve. This is the best way to begin an intermittent fasting schedule. You can slowly add an hour a day to your fasting window as you grow accustomed to eating this way. This method is fairly easy to stick to, and thus great for beginners, but may not be optimal for weight loss.

16–8 Fast

As you become comfortable with fasting, you can increase your fasting window to sixteen hours. A common approach to this fast is to eat your first meal of the day at noon and finish your last meal at 8 pm. After 8 pm you would consume nothing but calorie-free liquids until the next day at noon. You can pick the meal times that work best for you with this method as long as you are fasting for sixteen hours and keeping your eating window within the remaining eight hours.

5–2 Fast

This approach to intermittent fasting is daily rather than hourly; it involves eating regularly for five days of the week and then drastically restricting calorie intake for the other two days. This is a popular method of intermittent fasting because you can eat normally for five days of the week without having to change your routine. On the other two days, you restrict your calorie intake to 25% of your regular daily intake. The term "fasting" is a little misleading; you are still eating on your fasting days, just a limited amount. With this method, it is important that your fasting days are not consecutive because you need to give your body the calories and nutrients it needs to function optimally.

Alternate Day Fasting

This approach involves fasting every other day. It is similar to the 5–2 method; on fasting days you limit your calorie consumption to about 25% of your usual intake and on your regular, non-fasting days you eat normally. Some stricter approaches to this method say that you should consume no calories on your fasting days, but this is very severe and is not usually recommended.

Overall, it is important to remain consistent with whichever method you choose. You can try the different fasting times and approaches to decide which one feels most natural to you and which one you will be able to commit to in the long term. While every method can be effective, it really comes down to which one works best for you. No matter which type of approach you choose, the most important thing is to ensure that you are consuming high-quality foods packed full of nutrients when you are actually eating.

Importance of Physical Activity

High-Intensity Interval Training (HIIT)

Exercise is crucial for optimal liver health. It is essential for weight loss, which you should know by now has a very positive impact on liver health; basically, the more weight you lose, the healthier your liver will become. Moving in any way will be beneficial to your liver health, but certain forms of physical activity are more effective than others at reducing fat cells in the liver.

One of the most effective forms of exercise to target a fatty liver is High-Intensity Interval Training (most commonly known as HIIT). HIIT can be described as any workout that alternates between intense bursts of physical activity and periods of less intense activity. It usually involves several minutes of intense movements followed by lower-intensity recovery periods.

HIIT workouts can definitely pack a punch; they are far more effective in shorter amounts of time than a typical, moderate form of exercise. You can get an extremely beneficial workout in as little as ten minutes. A typical HIIT workout can last between 10–30 minutes and includes a variety of different forms of exercise.

The biggest key to your HIIT workouts being effective, however, is how *intense* your intense intervals actually are. You cannot just give 50% of your energy during these periods; this form of workout is designed for you to work as hard as you can. Premise of this form of exercise is that you are challenging yourself to expend the maximum amount of energy possible, and then mixing these bursts of intensity with periods of recovery.

Benefits of HITT

In addition to reducing liver fat, HIIT has many other extremely useful and attractive benefits.

1. It Is Efficient

HIIT workouts are one of the most effective workouts for anyone who has very limited time to exercise. The average workout takes between 20–30 minutes, but they can be extremely effective in as little as 10 minutes. You can get more benefits from a HIIT workout in 10–15 minutes than you can from an entire hour of jogging. It is also one of the most effective ways to get your heart rate up and tap into the fat-burning zone.

2. You Can Work Out Anywhere

The hallmark of HIIT is simply short bursts of intense exercise that get your heart rate up, so any type of exercise can qualify. Whether it is sprinting, swimming, jump roping, playing tennis, squat jumps, or burpees, as long as it gets your heart rate up fast, it qualifies. You do not need any equipment, and you can modify workouts to fit any time or space constraints you have. This means that even when you are traveling, stuck in your office at work, or at home while the kids are taking a nap, you can still work out effectively. With HITT there are no barriers to getting into shape and losing weight.

3. Your Body Will Become a Fat-Burning Machine

HIIT workouts are ideal for burning fat and building lean muscle (which continues the cycle of burning even more fat). The anaerobic part of HIIT workouts forces your body to use energy from stored fats, instead of carbohydrates, which makes fat-burning more efficient. You will continue burning fat long after you are done exercising for the day because the intense exertion keeps your body in fat-burning mode.

4. Your Metabolism Will Increase

Not only will your fat burning be kicked into high gear, but also your metabolism will also increase due to the stimulation of the production of Human Growth Hormone (HGH). HGH spikes after a HIIT workout, which increases your metabolism and your overall metabolic rate. This, in turn, improves insulin resistance and leads to weight loss. A healthy metabolic system will also help you get rid of toxins from your liver more efficiently and eliminate them from your body. These metabolic effects will last for hours after you have finished your HITT workout.

Simple HIIT Workouts You Can Do Anywhere

Here are some examples of simple workouts that can be done in your living room, your backyard, a local park, or even a hotel room if you are traveling. They require little to no equipment and not much space at all.

Jump Rope Interval Workout

Directions: Complete the following circuit four times, resting for one min in between each round.

1. Jump rope—1 minute
2. Push-ups from your knees—20 to 30 repetitions
3. Mountain climbers—45 repetitions (count each time your knee comes towards your elbow as one rep)
4. Plank—1 minute
5. High knees—30 seconds

Lower-Body Interval Workout

Directions: Complete the following circuit four times, resting for one min after the calf raises in each round. This is best suited to a backyard or a park.

1. Sprint—30 seconds
2. Squat jumps—45 seconds
3. Lunges—20 for each leg
4. Calf Raises—50 repetitions
5. Skater Jumps—10 for each leg

Burpee Interval Workout

Directions: Complete the following circuit four times, resting for one min after the burpees in each round.

1. Push-ups—as many repetitions as possible in 30 seconds
2. Jumping Jacks—60 repetitions
3. Burpees—20 repetitions

20-Minute AMRAP

Directions: Complete As Many Rounds as Possible (AMRAP) within 20 minutes.

1. Reverse lunges—10 for each leg
2. Bear crawl—travel 15 ft
3. Walking lunges—10 for each leg
4. Squat jumps—15 repetitions

Will HIIT Heal a Fatty Liver?

As you can see, these workouts can be done by anyone, anywhere. You don't have to spend a lot of money on a gym membership; you can find thousands of videos online to follow, or you can stick to the simple exercises that I have included here. Start slowly, build up your endurance, and I truly believe that you will amaze yourself with what you can accomplish. As your workouts get easier for you, challenge yourself to work harder or to do more difficult exercises. Your confidence will soar as you get stronger, feel better, have more energy, and begin to lose weight. While exercise alone will not deliver all of the healing results your liver needs, it is definitely one of the key pieces of the puzzle. When you pair physical activity with optimal nutrition, plenty of sleep, and stress reduction, you will transform your body, your health, and your energy. You have the power to unlock the healthy version of yourself that has been hiding all of this time. By transforming your workout routine, your nutrition, and even your stress levels, you will be transforming your life for good as well.

Chapter 4. The Importance of Following a Well-Defined Diet

Dietary Approaches to Treating a Fatty Liver

To treat fatty liver disease, you must make long-term dietary modifications rather than sporadic alterations. According to major gastroenterology and public health experts, sustainable changes are the most crucial element. For the most part, a diet high in fruits, vegetables, and nuts is the most effective way to combat fatty liver. Others are:

- A little amount of salt and sugar
- Animal products have just a very small amount of saturated fats
- No alcoholic beverages consumption
- Whole Grains

The Healthy Fatty Liver diet is by the American Liver Foundation as a calorie-restrictive way to lose weight. When it comes to your plate of food, experts in the field recommend half fruits and vegetables, one-quarter protein, and the other quarter starchy carbohydrates.

To reduce fatty liver, follow these two simple rules: Go for low-calorie, Mediterranean-style meals instead. Do your best to eat a wide variety of plant-based and whole-grain meals and extra-virgin olive oil, fish, chicken, and cheese in moderation. Avoid processed meats, refined carbohydrates, and added sugars. Fatal liver disease may be cured by decreasing 7 to 10 percent of your body weight.

Diet Guide for Various Fatty Liver Conditions

Alcoholic Liver Disease (ALD)

If you are drinking much or have been drinking alcohol excessively, this is the first stage of injury to your liver due to the buildup of fatty deposits. If proper care is taken and you stay away from alcohol, this can be completely reversed. As per the studies, only 20% of people with alcohol-related fatty liver go on to develop inflammation (alcoholic hepatitis) and eventually cirrhosis.

People who have been drinking alcohol excessively and have alcoholic liver damage have been found most of the time malnourished or undernourished which means their body lacks in nutrients that it requires to function properly. This lack of nourishment could be due to several factors, some common ones are:

- If you are not eating well and just drinking, you are asking your body to work hard to process alcohol. Alcohol has no nutritional value but requires a lot of energy for the body to process it.
- Poor or unbalanced diet.
- Loss of appetite due to heavy drinking. If you are drinking as well as smoking, the condition will become worse. Smoking is known for suppressing hunger.
- Poor absorption of food nutrients as the liver is less able to produce bile to aid digestion.

You could be undernourished even if you are overweight. It all relates to what and how you eat. If you eat well and still becoming overweight, get yourself checked, if you have not already. This condition could be due to fluid retention.

You should be prescribed vitamin B if you have been drinking excessively or at harmful levels. People with alcoholic liver disease generally lack the vitamin called thiamin, which is a vitamin B that helps your body to convert carbohydrates into energy. Consult your doctor or dietitian if this has not been prescribed.

For people with alcoholic liver disease, the most important change in the diet is to stop drinking alcohol and start eating a well-balanced diet. For affected patients, eating a well-balanced diet with enough proteins and carbohydrates is a must.

Non Alcoholic Fatty Liver Disease (NAFLD)

As the name suggests, non-alcoholic fatty liver disease is a condition when there is a buildup of fat in the liver cells even if the patient does not drink alcohol excessively. At the initial stages, the fat deposits may not trigger any symptoms but it has been found that in some cases, this may progress to inflammation called Nonalcoholic Steatohepatitis (NASH) which further can lead to scarring of the tissues in the liver and even cirrhosis.

People may think about what could be the cause of developing a fatty liver without excessive consumption of alcohol. There could be several factors or reasons for developing a fatty liver. You are most likely to develop a fatty liver if you:

- Have diabetes.
- Are overweight or obese.
- An insulin resistance body where your body does not respond to insulin as it should.
- Have high blood cholesterol.

You might be advised to work on some changes to your diet and lifestyle if you have been diagnosed with non-alcoholic fatty liver disease. These diet and lifestyle changes include:

- Eating a lot of vegetables and fruits.
- Eating slow-release starchy foods, such as potatoes and bread.
- Doing regular exercises such as walking, jogging, or swimming.
- Reduce or stop the consumption of alcohol.
- Avoid refined sugars and saturated fats which are commonly found in chocolate, cakes, and biscuits.

Acute Viral Hepatitis

People who have acute hepatitis, also known as short-term hepatitis, caused by a virus like hepatitis, should continue to eat a normal diet. In some cases, it is found that patients lose some weight in this condition. In a situation like this, a patient may need extra nutrition to prevent unplanned weight loss. Higher energy and higher protein diet are recommended for such patients. A dietitian can advise on this.

Chronic Viral Hepatitis

If you suffer from a long-term hepatitis infection caused by a virus such as hepatitis B or hepatitis C that lasts for more than six to seven months, the condition is called Chronic Viral Hepatitis. In such a condition, it is also recommended to eat a normal well-balanced diet. Fasting due for any reason is not recommended at all if you have chronic liver disease.

It is highly recommended to maintain an appropriate weight as per your height and build because it has been found in studies that more weight can increase and speed up the damages caused by hepatitis C and can slow down the recovery.

Some studies show that some people have conditions like poor appetite, nausea, vomiting, and unintentional loss of weight during the treatment with anti-viral agents. If all or any of these conditions last for more than a few days, you must consult a doctor immediately.

Autoimmune Hepatitis

Autoimmune hepatitis is also categorized as chronic liver disease in which the body's immune system attacks the normal cells and components of the liver and causes inflammation and liver damage. In a condition like this, sometimes, patients have been prescribed steroids. In some cases, patients prescribed steroids find that their appetite increases over time and they gradually start gaining weight.

If you are suffering from autoimmune hepatitis and on steroids and have symptoms like an increase in appetite and weight gain, it is still important and recommended to eat a well-balanced diet. If you are on steroids for a long time, it is important that you have been prescribed vitamin D and calcium by your doctor.

If however, you start gaining more weight and it does not seem to slow down, you should try to reduce foods high in calories such as:

- Sugar
- Cakes
- Fried food
- Pies and crisps
- Biscuits
- Chocolate
- Sweets
- Pasties

It is also recommended that you use low-fat milk and spreads and eat more fruit and vegetables. If it still increases, you must consult your doctor or dietician immediately.

Haemochromatosis

Haemochromatosis, also known as inherited iron overload disorder, is a condition where your body absorbs more iron than normal. It is not recommended to make any specific dietary changes in this condition and the patient should continue to eat a well-balanced diet.

If you are diagnosed with Haemochromatosis, it is recommended to avoid iron supplements or multivitamins with iron. You should also avoid foods that are enriched with iron like some breakfast cereals and drinks.

You need to be cautious if you are taking vitamin C in the form of a pill, as these pills are known to increase the absorption of iron. On the other hand, vitamin C from vegetables and fruit can be taken. You should also make sure that your alcohol intake is minimum as alcohol can speed up liver damage and may increase iron absorption.

Wilson's Disease

Wilson disease is a condition where your liver cannot metabolize enough copper and remove it from your body. Generally, it is treated with the help of a copper chelating agent, like penicillamine, which aid bind copper and removes it.

In most cases, you will be prescribed to take vitamin B supplements, if you are treated with penicillamine because penicillamine can increase your body's need for vitamin B. People suffering from Wilson's disease should know that most foods contain copper and some foods contain it in large amounts. Some examples of food that contain a high amount of copper are:

- Chocolate
- Shellfish
- Mushrooms
- Offal
- Nuts

If you are taking your medications and your body is responding well to them, it has been seen that doctors rarely suggest avoiding these foods.

It is a good practice to ask your doctor if you require supplements. It has been found in the studies that some people with Wilson's disease may also be treated with zinc, as zinc can block the absorption of copper from food in the intestine.

Gilbert's Syndrome

Gilbert's syndrome (GS) is a condition where the amount of bilirubin in your blood is higher than normal. If you do suffer from Gilbert's syndrome, always avoid dieting or fasting because they might increase the levels of bilirubin in your blood and also dehydrate you.

It is important and highly recommended that you continue to eat regularly and healthily, and also drink plenty of water. In some studies, it has been found that some people cannot tolerate the intake of carbohydrate foods such as rice, pasta, potatoes, and bread. If you are one of them, it is recommended to have a high amount of protein in your diet.

Chapter 5. Foods Suitable for the Fatty Liver Diet

Foods to Enjoy

Legumes: Lentils, chickpeas, black beans, navy beans, pinto beans, kidney beans, and their relatives are among the most effective foods at helping control blood sugar and blood fat levels. These are also truly filling foods thanks to their uniquely high protein and fiber content.

Fruit: Fruits of all varieties are potent due to the large number of anti-inflammatory polyphenol compounds they contain, as well as rich amounts of fiber, vitamins, and minerals. Berries, oranges, apples, and bananas may be particularly beneficial, but when it comes to fruit, you really don't need to pick sides.

Veggies: Owing to vegetables' incredible capacity to improve health via fiber, vitamin, mineral, and antioxidant content, there is no question that vegetables must comprise an important part of your dietary strategy.

Non-starchy veggies: Zucchini, broccoli, Brussels sprouts, spinach, kale, bell peppers, carrots, asparagus, eggplant, Swiss chard, and cauliflower are among your many options.

Starchy veggies: Beets, sweet potatoes, and various types of squash are among the prime choices.

Lean meats (chicken, turkey—especially breast): Using very lean protein sources like chicken and turkey breast is a great way to provide protein without the saturated fat found in other meats.

Healthy fats (nuts, seeds, avocado, and certain oils): You can't go wrong in this category with foods containing healthy fats. Flax, chia, hemp seeds, and walnuts are unique among this group for their high omega-3 fat content.

Avocado and olive oil are also uniquely high in what is known as monounsaturated fats, which help lower cholesterol levels and have essentially the opposite effect of saturated fat in this regard. Almonds, pistachios, and cashews are other examples of foods high in this fat, and they also contain large amounts of fat-soluble vitamin E, which may be uniquely useful for good liver health.

Eggs: Despite what some think, eggs can be consumed regularly. As part of a balanced style of eating, their cholesterol content won't have a negative effect on our health.

Low/medium glycemic index grains: Choosing grains lower in glycemic index (GI) is a relevant consideration for those living with fatty liver, primarily due to the fact that insulin resistance and type 2 diabetes could play a role in the progression of the disease. Options in this category include steel-cut oatmeal, quinoa, whole-grain bread/pasta, and brown rice.

Soy: Soy-based foods such as tofu, tempeh, soy milk, and edamame offer an alternative protein source to help you lessen your reliance on saturated fat-rich animal proteins, which in turn improves liver health. Soy-based foods also have a unique cholesterol-lowering effect.

Low-fat dairy: This includes products like kefir and yogurt that contain probiotics.

Seafood/fish: Fatty varieties such as salmon, mackerel, trout, tuna, and sardines are particularly high in one or both vitamin D and omega-3 fatty acids.

Foods to Limit

These foods should play a lesser role than the foods to enjoy freely, as it relates to your dietary pattern.

- **Refined carbohydrates:** These are foods made primarily from white flour such as white bread/bagels, and most types of store-bought baked goods like pretzels, muffins, and cakes.
  Although not technically considered "refined" carbohydrates, certain commonly available foods like various types of russet potatoes as well as instant oatmeal are high in glycemic index and may not be the best choices for regular consumption, especially in those with type 2 diabetes.
- **Saturated fats:** Saturated fats are highest in all types of red meat, ranging from beef to lamb, and pork to darker-meat poultry. Saturated fats are also high in dairy-based products like mayonnaise, butter, cheese, and high-fat yogurt. Coconut oil is also uniquely high in saturated fat among cooking oils and, although it acts differently in the body, it may be important to moderate for those with fatty liver disease.

Foods to Be Avoided

With fatty liver disease, foods to avoid are typically those that can cause a spike in blood sugar levels and lead to weight gain. This includes the following foods:

- **Sugary beverages including soda and juice:** The main enemies of the liver are carbohydrates and sugars. Consuming too much high-fructose corn syrup and refined sugar that are present in soda and sugary beverages can cause a fatty buildup in the liver.
- **Low-calorie diet drinks:** Some people turn to sugar substitutes thinking that it is better for their health. However, sugar in any form is the single most important cause of obesity and can also damage the liver.
- **Butter and ghee:** Butter and ghee won't hurt the liver when taken in moderation. However, these foods are high in saturated fat and have been linked to high triglycerides in the liver. If you're ever going to use butter or ghee in your cooking, use them sparingly.
- **Sweet baked products:** Again, sugar in all its forms is bad for the liver. This includes cakes, ice cream, pastries, and pies. These foods are high in sugary carbs and are detrimental to your success if you are trying to keep your liver healthy.
- **Fatty meats, cured meats, sausages, and bacon:** All these foods are high in saturated fats and could contribute to fatty liver disease. Avoid them at all costs or eat them in moderate amounts if you want to maintain a healthy liver.
- **Alcohol:** Any form of alcohol is not recommended for people who have fatty liver disease as a result of excessive alcohol consumption. Drinking alcohol even in small amounts may lead to serious liver damage if you already have liver disease. However, you can drink a glass of wine once in a while if you have NAFLD.
- **Salty foods:** Research suggests that eating food high in salt can worsen the symptoms of NAFLD. One reason is that salty foods often accompany foods high in calories or high in fat. Another reason is that salty foods can cause dysregulation of the renin-angiotensin system. This usually increases one's risk of getting fatty liver disease.
- **Fried foods:** Fried foods are often rich in calories and are not good for people with liver disease.

Chapter 6. Importance of Having a Healthy Liver

As the largest organ in our body, our liver has three broad, essential tasks that are crucial to our body functioning properly: detoxification, synthesis, and storage.

Under these broad categories, the liver is actually responsible for more than 500 different functions. I will explain in depth how some of these functions are related to essential digestion and metabolism, detoxification, immunity, and the storage of nutrients within the body.

Digestion and Metabolism

Anything that is consumed through the mouth (food, medicine, supplements, alcohol, and even toxins) gets filtered by the liver after it has been digested by the stomach and the small intestines. The liver then processes nutrients so that they can be utilized by the rest of the body.

The cells of the liver (hepatocytes) produce a substance called bile, a mixture of water, bile salts, cholesterol, and bilirubin, that plays an important role in the digestive process. Bile is a greenish-brown, thick substance that passes through bile ducts to be stored in the gallbladder until a meal containing fat is eaten. The gallbladder is then signaled to release the bile into the first part of the small intestines (the duodenum). There the bile emulsifies the fat, making it easier for the body to digest and absorb it.

The liver is also able to convert simple sugars in the bloodstream into glycogen, which is better for storage. This makes the liver an energy center for the body because it helps control the fine balance of simple and complex sugar storage and controls the release of sugar stores when the body needs them for energy.

In addition to utilizing bile to help process fats and being able to convert simple sugars into glycogen, the liver also plays an important role in the digestion and processing of proteins by helping to create some of the essential building blocks that form protein, known as amino acids. Amino acids are essential for many vital chemical reactions. They are transported to the liver during digestion and most of the body's protein is synthesized here. If there is too much protein, amino acids can then be converted into fat and stored or made into glucose for energy.

The liver's hepatocytes perform numerous essential metabolic functions that support the body's cells. The majority of the blood leaving the digestive system flows through the portal vein and into the liver. This is what allows for the metabolizing of carbohydrates, fats, and proteins into material for the body to utilize.

Detoxification

When blood flows from the small intestines, spleen, and pancreas into the liver through the hepatic portal vein, the cells of the liver are on constant watch for any potentially toxic substances. If detected, they produce enzymes to metabolize these toxins, such as drugs and alcohol, into inactive metabolites that can then be removed through waste. The liver will also metabolize excess hormones that have been produced by the body and remove them from circulation through waste.

After these harmful substances have been broken down and made inactively, the remaining by-products are excreted into the bile to be sent to the intestines and eliminated as feces, or into the blood to be filtered by the kidneys and eliminated as urine.

Immunity

The liver plays an important role in immunity. It is designed to detect pathogens entering the body through the intestines and to isolate and remove bacteria, viruses, or other infectious organisms that may be present in our food. This puts it at the forefront of our body's immune response.

The liver has the largest collection of phagocytic cells in the body. Phagocytes are cells that protect the body by ingesting harmful foreign particles, bacteria, and dead or dying cells. These phagocytes make the liver the body's frontline defense and allow it to mount a rapid and robust immune response to protect our bodies from foreign pathogens. So much blood passes through the hepatic portal system that the liver cells are able to clean a large volume of blood very quickly. Dynamic interactions between a large number of immune cells in the liver are key to maintaining balance and overall tissue health.

Storage

The liver provides the storage for many essential nutrients, vitamins, and minerals that are obtained from digestion. Our liver is able to store vitamins A, D, E, and K, which are all fat-soluble vitamins, along with vitamins B-12, iron, and copper. By storing these essential nutrients, the liver is able to provide a constant supply to all of the tissues of the body. The reserves are released into the bloodstream from the liver when additional amounts of these important nutrients are needed.

In addition to the storage of these nutrients, the liver is also able to convert excess glucose into glycogen to store for later energy use. Glucose is the main source of energy for our cells. When the body needs additional fuel and it has not received it from current food sources, the body sends a signal for the stored glycogen to be broken down to release glucose back into the bloodstream where it can be used as fuel for the cells.

Other Important Functions of the Liver

While we have touched on the main functions of the liver, this incredible organ actually performs more than 500 functions, some of which scientists do not yet fully understand and are continually researching to learn more about.

Some additional responsibilities include:

- Regulating blood clotting
- Producing certain proteins for blood plasma
- Converting poisonous ammonia into urea to be removed as waste
- Producing special proteins to help carry fats through the body
- Producing cholesterol which is used to make vitamin D

All of these functions show that you cannot underestimate the importance of the liver and how essential it is to good health. It is a gatekeeper to any threats that your body may encounter and therefore needs to be cared for properly. Any signs of liver issues should be addressed immediately to put your body back on a path to optimal health.

Causes of Fatty Liver

NAFLD is characterized by the excessive presence of stored fat in and around the liver, which occurs when the liver's ability to transport and utilize fatty acids in the body is compromised by factors other than alcohol consumption. Scientists are not 100 percent clear on the full causes of NAFLD, although the following are considered relevant considerations:

- **High blood cholesterol and blood triglyceride levels:** There is considerable evidence that these are major contributors to a fatty liver disease diagnosis.
- **Polycystic Ovary Syndrome (PCOS):** Individuals living with PCOS are believed to be at elevated risk for NAFLD.
- **Hypothyroidism:** Individuals with a history of hypothyroidism may also be at an increased risk.
- **Genetics and other personal factors:** Family/genetic history and the use of certain medications may also play a role.

Symptoms

One notable symptom, in both early and later stages of fatty liver disease, is upper-right abdominal pain. It sometimes begins as an inconsistent, dull ache or fullness, but as liver disease progresses, this pain can become more severe. You may also notice that you have stubborn weight gain around your abdomen that does not disappear no matter what you do, what you eat, or how much you exercise. But exercising will become increasingly difficult as a result of the fatigue that is associated with fatty liver disease. This fatigue might increase gradually until you find that you are struggling just to get through the day. Read on. You can get your energy back!

Many symptoms will initially seem vague and not obviously related to liver health when you are evaluating how you feel on a day-to-day basis. If you do have symptoms, they may include:

- Fatigue
- Jaundice
- Weight loss
- Loss of appetite
- Nausea
- Vomiting
- Confusion
- Trouble concentrating
- Pain in the center or upper-right part of the belly
- Enlarged liver
- Bloating and gas
- Constipation
- Pale or dark tar-colored stool
- Dry and dark patches on the neck and under the arms
- Swelling in the legs and ankles
- Weakness
- Excessive sweating
- Bruising easily
- Dark urine.

These symptoms might increase in severity as the disease progresses. The bad news is that once your symptoms have advanced, you are in the latter and far more dangerous stages of liver disease. Once the disease reaches this point, addressing, repairing, and healing the damage becomes far more difficult without medical intervention.

Problems

Depending on several factors, including lifestyle intervention, simple fatty liver can progress to NASH. With more time and increased liver damage, this could lead to severe inflammation (fibrosis) and eventually severe liver damage (cirrhosis).

Severe liver damage could warrant a liver transplant, and NAFLD, even if only moderate in severity, increases one's risk for cardiovascular disease—the number one cause of death in the United States.

Common Comorbidities

Because NAFLD is strongly associated with insulin resistance and elevated blood fat levels (cholesterol, triglycerides), it's not uncommon for those living with the condition to also be dealing with comorbidities such as type 2 diabetes, metabolic syndrome, PCOS, and more.

- **Type 2 Diabetes:** Type 2 diabetes is a condition characterized by blood sugar levels that remain above the optimal range in both the short and long term. Insulin resistance is one of several potential drivers of diabetes because insulin is the hormone that allows blood sugar to enter the cells for use. When our cells don't respond to insulin as they should, blood sugar levels can elevate.
- **Metabolic syndrome:** Metabolic syndrome speaks to multiple simultaneous abnormalities across important parameters such as blood sugar, blood pressure, cholesterol, and/or triglycerides. The elevation of one or more of these markers can increase one's risk for a variety of conditions including heart disease. Those with metabolic syndrome may be at higher risk for NAFLD as compared to someone with these markers in check.
- **Polycystic Ovary Syndrome (PCOS):** PCOS is a multifactorial condition, and its diagnosis is based on the presence of specific criteria such as cysts in the ovaries, elevated androgen levels, and insulin resistance. Once again, insulin resistance is the factor that ties NAFLD and PCOS together on a physiological level.
- **Cardiovascular disease:** Individuals living with fatty liver disease may be at increased risk of cardiovascular disease, especially since some of the key dietary considerations for fatty liver are also strongly related to cardiovascular health.
- **Various other conditions:** Sexual health issues, sleep apnea, and osteoporosis may likely occur in those living with NAFLD. The physiological abnormalities associated with liver disease affect multiple bodily systems, including the bones and reproductive organs.

Chapter 7. Complications When NAFLD Is Ignored

NASH

When NAFLD is left untreated, the damage can progress to steatosis with inflammation and hepatocyte necrosis (death of liver cells). This condition is commonly referred to as NASH. This occurs when your liver starts to lose function and begins to interfere with your ability to metabolize certain foods and medication. NASH is heavily influenced by daily lifestyle. Excessive calorie intake on a regular basis and a lack of physical activity are large contributors to the development of this disease and differ from fatty liver disease caused by alcohol or medication abuse.

Symptoms eventually progress in severity and become more attributable to liver disease as NASH becomes more advanced. Some signs to watch out for include muscle weakness; internal bleeding in the esophagus, stomach, and intestines; a buildup of fluid in the body (particularly in the abdomen); severe yellowing of the skin and eyes; and eventually even liver failure.

The most definitive way to correctly diagnose NASH is with a liver biopsy. As mentioned before, this is the best way to truly identify what stage of liver disease is present even if it is slightly more invasive and more expensive than some other forms of testing.

Fibrosis

When the liver disease has progressed to NASH, the inflammation in the liver cells can lead to scarring in the liver called fibrosis.

Inflammation is a persistent cycle when you have liver disease. As a result of the inflammation, your body is constantly trying to repair the damaged cells in the liver by continually depositing collagen. However, the signal that a healthy liver would give to stop depositing collagen is interrupted because of the inflammation, so it continues to deposit more collagen beyond what is needed. All of that extra collagen begins to stiffen around the liver tissue. This build-up of collagen, and other proteins, causing scar tissue formation is called fibrosis. The scar tissue and regenerative nodules that are the result of the inflammation and fibrosis of NASH will replace healthy liver tissue and prevent the liver from functioning normally.

If detected early enough, fibrosis can be reversed through dietary and lifestyle changes, and the underlying liver disease that caused the development of fibrosis can be cured or treated. If fibrosis is left untreated, however, it can lead to cirrhosis and liver cancer.

Cirrhosis

When the scarring on the liver becomes more severe and the damage is permanent, it is typically diagnosed as cirrhosis. While most people immediately think of cirrhosis as a result of alcohol consumption, it is actually just as common in NAFLD.

When liver damage is still in the stages of fibrosis, before it has advanced to cirrhosis, it is still reversible. However, there becomes a point where there is too much damage and the liver is beyond the point of being able to repair itself. As cirrhosis causes continued damage to the liver, excessive scar formation results in further loss of liver function and thus an increased risk of liver cancer and liver failure. At this point, medical intervention may be necessary in order to prevent liver failure.

Liver Cancer

If cirrhosis advances far enough, one of the main complications is liver cancer. Liver cancer is the growth and spread of unhealthy cells in the liver. It is a leading cause of cancer-related deaths worldwide, but especially in the United States. While other common cancers have seen an improvement in survival rates, liver cancer deaths continue to increase at an alarming rate.

It is rare to develop liver cancer without first having cirrhosis. This makes it especially important to receive regular testing and monitoring for liver cancer once you have been diagnosed with more advanced fibrosis or cirrhosis. The best survival chances occur when liver cancer is detected, diagnosed, and treated as early as possible.

Liver Failure

In the advanced stages of liver disease, liver failure can occur. Liver failure happens when large portions of the liver are damaged beyond repair from severe scarring and inflammation. At this point, the liver cannot function any longer. The liver performs so many essential, life-sustaining functions that when it can no longer perform these effectively, it becomes a life-threatening condition that typically requires urgent medical care.

Liver failure usually happens gradually over many years and is the final stage of successive liver diseases; a liver transplant may be a patient's only option. However, a transplant is a very risky surgical procedure associated with various complications.

Prevention of Fatty Liver Disease

It's important to maintain a healthy lifestyle to avoid fatty liver disease and its repercussions.

- Managing your weight
- Eating a nutrient-rich diet low in saturated fats, trans fats, and refined carbohydrates
- Take steps to manage your blood sugar, triglyceride levels, as well as cholesterol levels
- Following your doctor's recommended treatment plan for diabetes if you have it
- Aiming for at least 30 minutes of exercise most days of the week

These actions may also assist you in enhancing your general health.

In many situations, fatty liver disease may be reversed by making lifestyle changes such as restricting alcohol intake, changing one's diet, and losing weight. These modifications may assist in avoiding additional liver injury and scarring. It's very vital for those with AFLD to completely avoid alcohol. Consider enrolling in a detoxification program and counseling if you need assistance quitting drinking.

In general, the prognosis for fatty liver disease is better when treated early on, before fibrosis and Cirrhosis develop. It's important to stick to your doctor's treatment plan and live a healthy lifestyle to get the greatest results.

The next chapter will contain recipes suitable for your fatty liver.

Chapter 8. Drink and Smoothie Recipes

1. Lettuce, Banana, and Berries Smoothie

Preparation time: 5 minutes

Cooking time: 0 minutes

Servings: 2

Ingredients:

- 1/2 burro banana
- 1/4 cup blueberries
- 1 cup Romaine lettuce
- 2 tbsp key lime juice
- 1/2 cup soft jelly coconut water

Directions:

1. Plug in a high-speed food processor or blender and add all the ingredients to its jar.
2. Cover the blender jar with its lid and then pulse for 40 to 60 seconds until smooth.
3. Divide the drink between two glasses and then serve.

Nutrition:

- Calories: 147
- Fat: 0.8 g
- Protein: 3.3 g
- Carbohydrates: 36 g
- Fiber: 4 g

2. Apple, Quinoa, and Fig Smoothie

Preparation time: 5 minutes

Cooking time: 0 minutes

Servings: 2

Ingredients:

- 1/2 cup cooked quinoa
- 1/2 large red apple, cored
- 1 cup amaranth greens
- 1 fig
- 1 tsp Bromide Plus Powder

Extra:

- 1 tbsp raisins
- 1 tbsp date
- 1 cup hemp seed milk, homemade

Directions:

1. Plug in a high-speed food processor or blender and add all the ingredients to its jar.
2. Cover the blender jar with its lid and then pulse for 40 to 60 seconds until smooth.
3. Divide the drink between two glasses and then serve.

Nutrition:

- Calories: 153
- Fat: 1 g
- Protein: 3 g
  Carbohydrates: 28 g, Fiber: 3 g

3. Strawberry Shake

Preparation time: 5 minutes

Cooking time: 10 minutes

Servings: 2

Ingredients:

- 1 cup strawberries
- 1/2 cup Brazil nuts, soaked
- 1 tbsp agave syrup
- 1/3 cup Irish Moss gel
- 1 1/2 cups spring water

Directions:

1. Plug in a high-speed food processor or blender and add all the ingredients to its jar.
2. Cover the blender jar with its lid and then pulse for 40 to 60 seconds until smooth.
3. Divide the drink between two glasses and then serve.

Nutrition:

- Calories: 137
- Fat: 5 g
- Protein: 1 g
- Carbohydrates: 22 g
- Fiber: 2 g

4. Sweet Sunrise Smoothie

Preparation time: 5 minutes

Cooking time: 0 minutes

Servings: 2

Ingredients:

- 1 cup mango chunks
- 1 cup raspberries
- 1/2 burro banana
- 1 orange, peeled
- 1 cup spring water

Directions:

1. Plug in a high-speed food processor or blender and add all the ingredients to its jar.
2. Cover the blender jar with its lid and then pulse for 40 to 60 seconds until smooth.
3. Divide the drink between two glasses and then serve.

Nutrition:

- Calories: 130
- Fat: 0 g
- Protein: 0 g
- Carbohydrates: 30 g
- Fiber: 3 g

5. Green Sea Moss Drink

Preparation time: 5 minutes

Cooking time: 0 minutes

Servings: 2

Ingredients:

- 1 apple, cored, diced
- 2 cups kale
- 1 cup cucumber chunks
- 2 cups coconut water

Extra:

- 1 key lime, juiced
- 1 tbsp sea moss gel

Directions:

1. Plug in a high-speed food processor or blender and add all the ingredients to its jar.
2. Cover the blender jar with its lid and then pulse for 40 to 60 seconds until smooth.
3. Divide the drink between two glasses and then serve.

Nutrition:

- Calories: 156
- Fat: 1.8 g
- Protein: 9.4 g
- Carbohydrates: 32.8 g
- Fiber: 10.2 g

6. Banana Herbal Drink

Preparation time: 5 minutes

Cooking time: 0 minutes

Servings: 2

Ingredients:

- 2 burro bananas, peeled
- 1 cup herbal tea
- 1 tbsp agave syrup

Directions:

1. Plug in a high-speed food processor or blender and add all the ingredients to its jar.
2. Cover the blender jar with its lid and then pulse for 40 to 60 seconds until smooth.
3. Divide the drink between two glasses and then serve.

Nutrition:

- Calories: 177
- Fat: 1 g
- Protein: 2 g
- Carbohydrates: 40 g
- Fiber: 4 g

7. Watermelon, Cantaloupe, and Mango Smoothie

Preparation time: 5 minutes

Cooking time: 0 minutes

Servings: 2

Ingredients:

- 1/2 large mango, peeled
- 1/2 burro banana, peeled
- 1/2 cup cantaloupe, peeled
- 1/2 cup amaranth greens
- 1/2 cup watermelon chunks

Extra:

- 1 cup soft jelly coconut water

Directions:

1. Plug in a high-speed food processor or blender and add all the ingredients to its jar.
2. Cover the blender jar with its lid and then pulse for 40 to 60 seconds until smooth.
3. Divide the drink between two glasses and then serve.

Nutrition:

- Calories: 132
- Fat: 1 g
- Protein: 3.5 g
- Carbohydrates: 30.1 g
- Fiber: 3.2 g

8. BlackBerry and Banana Smoothie

Preparation time: 5 minutes

Cooking time: 0 minutes

Servings: 2

Ingredients:

- 1 burro banana, peeled
- 1/2 cup blackberries
- 2 dates, pitted
- 1 cup mango chunks
- 1/4 cup walnut milk, unsweetened

Extra:

- 3/4 cup coconut water

Directions:

1. Plug in a high-speed food processor or blender and add all the ingredients to its jar.
2. Cover the blender jar with its lid and then pulse for 40 to 60 seconds until smooth.
3. Divide the drink between two glasses and then serve.

Nutrition:

- Calories: 147.7
- Fat: 0.7 g
- Protein: 5 g
- Carbohydrates: 34 g
- Fiber: 4.1 g

9. Green Smoothie With Raspberries

Preparation time: 5 minutes

Cooking time: 10 minutes

Servings: 2

Ingredients:

- 1 cup raspberries
- 1 cup kale leaves
- 1 tbsp sea moss
- 2 tbsp key lime juice
- 1 cup soft-jelly coconut milk

Directions:

1. Plug in a high-speed food processor or blender and add all the ingredients to its jar.
2. Cover the blender jar with its lid and then pulse for 40 to 60 seconds until smooth.
3. Divide the drink between two glasses and then serve.

Nutrition:

- Calories: 151
- Fat: 1.2 g
- Protein: 3 g
- Carbohydrates: 37 g
- Fiber: 8 g

10. Veggie-Ful Smoothie

Preparation time: 5 minutes

Cooking time: 0 minutes

Servings: 2

Ingredients:

- 1 pear, cored, deseeded
- 1/2 cup watercress
- 1/4 of avocado, peeled
- 1/2 cup Romaine lettuce
- 1/2 of cucumber, peeled, deseeded

Extra:

- 1 tbsp date
- 1/2 cup spring water

Directions:

1. Plug in a high-speed food processor or blender and add all the ingredients to its jar.
2. Cover the blender jar with its lid and then pulse for 40 to 60 seconds until smooth.
3. Divide the drink between two glasses and then serve.

Nutrition:

- Calories: 145
- Fat: 6 g
- Protein: 1 g
- Carbohydrates: 25 g
- Fiber: 6 g

11. Apple Pie Smoothie

Preparation time: 5 minutes

Cooking time: 0 minutes

Servings: 2

Ingredients:

- 1/2 large apple, deseeded
- 1/4 cup walnuts
- 2 figs
- 1 tsp Bromide Plus Powder

Extra:

- 1 tbsp date

Directions:

1. Plug in a high-speed food processor or blender and add all the ingredients to its jar.
2. Cover the blender jar with its lid and then pulse for 40 to 60 seconds until smooth.
3. Divide the drink between two glasses and then serve.

Nutrition:

- Calories: 170
- Fat: 8 g
- Protein: 2 g
- Carbohydrates: 26 g
- Fiber: 8 g

12. Orange and Lettuce Smoothie

Preparation time: 5 minutes

Cooking time: 0 minutes

Servings: 2

Ingredients:

- 2 oranges, peeled, sliced
- 1 cup shredded lettuce, rinsed
- 2 apples, cored, sliced
- 1 cup spring water

Directions:

1. Plug in a high-speed food processor or blender and add all the ingredients to its jar.
2. Cover the blender jar with its lid and then pulse for 40 to 60 seconds until smooth.
3. Divide the drink between two glasses and then serve.

Nutrition:

- Calories: 140
- Fat: 0.9 g
- Protein: 1.3 g
- Carbohydrates: 31.8 g
- Fiber: 3 g

13. Green Tea and Lettuce Detox Smoothie

Preparation time: 5 minutes

Cooking time: 0 minutes

Servings: 2

Ingredients:

- 1/2 of burro banana
- 1/4 cup blueberries, fresh
- 1 cup Romaine lettuce
- 3 tbsp key lime juice

Extra:

- 1/2 cup soft jelly coconut water

Directions:

1. Plug in a high-speed food processor or blender and add all the ingredients to its jar.
2. Cover the blender jar with its lid and then pulse for 40 to 60 seconds until smooth.
3. Divide the drink between two glasses and then serve.

Nutrition:

- Calories: 134
- Fat: 4.5 g
- Protein: 4.6 g
- Carbohydrates: 20 g
- Fiber: 3.7 g

14. Chamomile Delight Smoothie

Preparation time: 5 minutes

Cooking time: 0 minutes

Servings: 2

Ingredients:

- 2 burro bananas, peeled
- 1/2 cup chamomile tea
- 1 tbsp date
- 1/2 cup walnut milk, homemade

Directions:

1. Plug in a high-speed food processor or blender and add all the ingredients to its jar.
2. Cover the blender jar with its lid and then pulse for 40 to 60 seconds until smooth.
3. Divide the drink between two glasses and then serve.

Nutrition:

- Calories: 142
- Fat: 5 g
- Protein: 3.5 g
- Carbohydrates: 25 g
- Fiber: 8.5 g

15. Honey Dew and Arugula Smoothie

Preparation time: 5 minutes

Cooking time: 0 minutes

Servings: 2

Ingredients:

- 1 large bunch of Calaloo
- 1 cup cucumber, deseeded
- 1 large bunch of arugula
- 1/4 cup honeydew pieces
- 1 pear, diced

Extra:

- 6 dates, pitted
- 1 tbsp sea moss gel
- 1/4 cup key lime juice
- 2 cups soft-jelly coconut water

Directions:

1. Plug in a high-speed food processor or blender and add all the ingredients to its jar.
2. Cover the blender jar with its lid and then pulse for 40 to 60 seconds until smooth.
3. Divide the drink between two glasses and then serve.

Nutrition:

- Calories: 189.5
- Fat: 2.5 g
- Protein: 1.5 g
- Carbohydrates: 42.6 g
- Fiber: 6.6 g

16. Watermelon and Strawberries Drink

Preparation time: 5 minutes

Cooking time: 0 minutes

Servings: 2

Ingredients:

- 1 cup strawberries
- 1 cup watermelon, chunks
- 1 tsp date
- 1 cup soft jelly coconut water

Directions:

1. Plug in a high-speed food processor or blender and add all the ingredients to its jar.
2. Cover the blender jar with its lid and then pulse for 40 to 60 seconds until smooth.
3. Divide the drink between two glasses and then serve.

Nutrition:

- Calories: 110
- Fat: 0 g
- Protein: 0 g
- Carbohydrates: 28 g
- Fiber: 6 g

17. Sweet Green Drink

Preparation time: 5 minutes

Cooking time: 10 minutes

Servings: 2

Ingredients:

- 1 cup greens
- 1 cucumber, peeled, deseeded
- 1 key lime, peeled
- 2 dates, pitted

Extra:

- 2 cups soft-jelly coconut water

Directions:

1. Plug in a high-speed food processor or blender and add all the ingredients to its jar.
2. Cover the blender jar with its lid and then pulse for 40 to 60 seconds until smooth.
3. Divide the drink between two glasses and then serve.

Nutrition:

- Calories: 112
- Fat: 0.1 g
- Protein: 0.3 g
- Carbohydrates: 27 g
- Fiber: 5 g

18. Banana Sea Moss Smoothie

Preparation time: 5 minutes

Cooking time: 0 minutes

Servings: 2

Ingredients:

- 1 cup kale
- 1/2 apple, cored, sliced
- 1 tsp sea moss
- 1/2 burro banana

Extra:

- 1 tsp Bromide Plus Powder

Directions:

1. Plug in a high-speed food processor or blender and add all the ingredients to its jar.
2. Cover the blender jar with its lid and then pulse for 40 to 60 seconds until smooth.
3. Divide the drink between two glasses and then serve.

Nutrition:

- Calories: 115
- Fat: 0.5 g
- Protein: 2 g
- Carbohydrates: 28 g
- Fiber: 2 g

19. Smoothie Bowl

Preparation time: 5 minutes

Cooking time: 0 minutes

Servings: 2

Ingredients:

- 1 burro banana, peeled
- 1 1/2 cup mixed berries
- 1 mango, peeled, destoned, chopped
- 2 tbsp walnut milk, homemade
- 1 tbsp walnut butter, homemade

Extra:

- 2 tbsp agave syrup

Directions:

1. Plug in a high-speed food processor or blender, add banana and berries, and then pulse at low speed until small pieces of fruits remain in the jar.
2. Add milk, butter, and agave syrup, pulse until combined, and then divide the mixture evenly between two bowls.
3. Top evenly with mango slices and some more berries and then serve.

Storage instructions: Divide the drink between two jars or bottles, cover it with a lid and then store the containers in the refrigerator for up to 3 days.

Nutrition:

- Calories: 338
- Fat: 9.6 g
- Protein: 8.6 g
- Carbohydrates: 64.6 g
- Fiber: 12.6 g

20. Refreshing Smoothie With Nuts

Preparation time: 5 minutes

Cooking time: 0 minutes

Servings: 2

Ingredients:

- 1/2 of burro banana, peeled
- 1/2 cup figs
- 2 strawberries
- 1/4 cup Brazil nuts
- 1 cup spring water

Directions:

1. Plug in a high-speed food processor or blender and add all the ingredients to its jar.
2. Cover the blender jar with its lid and then pulse for 40 to 60 seconds until smooth.
3. Divide the drink between two glasses and then serve.

Storage instructions: Divide the drink between two jars or bottles, cover it with a lid and then store the containers in the refrigerator for up to 3 days.

Nutrition:

- Calories: 234
- Fat: 2 g
- Protein: 6.1 g
- Carbohydrates: 53.1 g
- Fiber: 5.8 g

21. Cantaloupe Smoothie Tea

Preparation time: 5 minutes

Cooking time: 0 minutes

Servings: 2

Ingredients:

- 1 cantaloupe, peeled, deseeded, sliced
- 1/2 cup Herbal Tea
- 1/2 of burro banana, peeled
- 1/2 cup soft-jelly coconut water

Directions:

1. Plug in a high-speed food processor or blender and add all the ingredients to its jar.
2. Cover the blender jar with its lid and then pulse for 40 to 60 seconds until smooth.
3. Divide the drink between two glasses and then serve.

Storage instructions: Divide the drink between two jars or bottles, cover with a lid and then store the containers in the refrigerator for up to 3 days.

Nutrition:

- Calories: 114.7
- Fat: 0.6 g
- Protein: 1.8 g
- Carbohydrates: 27.8 g
- Fiber: 1 g

22. Watermelon Juice

Preparation time: 5 minutes

Cooking time: 0 minutes

Servings: 2

Ingredients

- 1 watermelon, peeled, deseeded, cubed
- 1 tbsp date sugar
- 1/2 of key lime, juiced, zest
- 2 cups soft-jelly coconut water

Directions

1. Place watermelon pieces in a high-speed food processor or blender, add lime zest and juice, add date sugar and then pulse until smooth.
2. Take two tall glasses, fill them with watermelon mixture until two-thirds full, and then pour in coconut water.
3. Stir until mixed and then serve.

Storage instructions: Divide the drink between two jars or bottles, cover it with a lid and then store the containers in the refrigerator for up to 3 days.

Nutrition:

- Calories: 55
- Fat: 1.3 g

- Protein: 0.9 g
- Carbohydrates: 9.9 g
- Fiber: 7 g

23. Green Smoothie

Preparation time: 5 minutes

Cooking time: 0 minutes

Servings: 2

Ingredients:

- 1 cup dandelion greens
- 1/2 cucumber, deseeded
- 1 apple, cored, deseeded
- 1 burro banana, peeled
- 1/2 tbsp walnuts

Extra:

- 1/2 tsp Bromide Plus Powder
- 1 cup soft-jelly coconut milk

Directions

1. Plug in a high-speed food processor or blender and add all the ingredients to its jar.
2. Cover the blender jar with its lid and then pulse for 40 to 60 seconds until smooth.
3. Divide the drink between two glasses and then serve.

Storage instructions: Divide the drink between two bottles or jars, cover it with their lids, and then store the containers in the refrigerator for up to 3 days.

Nutrition:

- Calories: 317
- Fat: 11.7 g
- Protein: 10 g
- Carbohydrates: 42 g
- Fiber: 7 g

Chapter 9. Breakfast Recipes

24. Liver Detox Smoothie

Preparation time: 10 minutes

Cooking time: 0 minutes

Servings: 2

Ingredients:

- 1 banana, peeled ripe
- 1/2 green apple, cored and chopped
- 1 carrot, medium-sized peeled and chopped
- 1 Baby spinach handful
- 1 (1/4-inch) nub turmeric root, peeled
- 1 tbsp fresh parsley, chopped
- 3 walnut halves
- 2 tbsp hemp protein powder
- 1/2 lemon, juiced
- 1 cinnamon, pinch optional
- 3/4 cup unsweetened almond milk

Directions:

1. In a blender, combine all the smoothie's ingredients and blend till it the completely smooth. Taste the smoothie and adjust the flavor with extra cinnamon and honey as desired.

Nutrition:

- Calories: 217
- Fat: 3 g
- Protein: 5 g
- Carbohydrates: 48 g

25. High Protein French Toast

Preparation time: 5 minutes

Cooking time: 15 minutes

Servings: 3

Ingredients:

- 6 bread slices
- 3 eggs
- 1/3 cup almond or rice milk
- Cooking spray
- 1 tbsp Olive oil

Directions:

1. Mix eggs, milk, and olive oil, and add cooking spray by warming the skillet.
2. Lay the bread in this egg mixture for 2 seconds. Please turn it on to coat the other side.
3. Plop it on the pan and turn it when it becomes golden brown.

Nutrition:

- Calories: 370
- Fat: 17 g
- Protein: 32 g
- Carbohydrates: 49 g

26. Broccoli Salad

Preparation time: 5 minutes

Cooking time: 5 minutes

Servings: 4

Ingredients:

- 1 head broccoli
- 1 tbsp butter or olive oil
- 2 tbsp heaped pomegranate seeds
- 1/2 red chili
- 2 nuts handfuls

Directions:

1. Place the broccoli in a serving dish after steaming until just soft.
2. Stir in butter or oil.
3. Mix with the remaining ingredients and serve.

Nutrition:

- Calories: 196.4
- Fat: 13.2 g
- Protein: 6.2 g
- Carbohydrates: 16.3 g

27. Classic Eggs Benedict With Lemon Basil Hollandaise

Preparation time: 25 minutes

Cooking time: 25 minutes

Servings: 4

Ingredients:

- 3 large eggs, divided
- 1/3 cup buttermilk
- 1 tsp arrowroot powder
- 1/2 tsp fresh lemon juice
- 1/2 tsp safflower oil
- 1/8 tsp ground cayenne pepper
- 1 tbsp fresh basil, chopped
- 2 (1 oz) all-natural slices turkey bacon
- 2 1/2-inch-thick vine tomato slices
- 1 English muffin, whole grain halved and toasted

Directions:

1. Prepare the sauce as follows: 1 egg, arrowroot, buttermilk, lemon juice, oil, and cayenne pepper in a small skillet over medium heat. Lower the heat to low and cook, often mixing, for 15 minutes or until thickened. Add 1 tbsp basil.
2. Meanwhile, poach eggs: Bring 2 inches of water to a simmer in a medium saucepan. In a small cup, crack 1 egg. Swirl the water with a spoon and gently add the egg, tucking the egg white close to the yolk with the spoon. Fill a small cup halfway with water and crack the remaining egg; repeat the tucking motion with the egg white. Cook for 4 minutes for each egg. Remove the eggs from the water using a slotted spoon.
3. In the meanwhile, heat a small nonstick skillet over high heat. Cook, flipping once, until bacon is crisp, approximately 4 minutes on each side. Remove the bacon from the pan and cut each piece in half; return the bacon to the skillet and sear for 1 to 2 minutes, flipping once. Divide the bacon, tomato, egg, and hollandaise between the English muffin halves. Additional basil may be used as a garnish.

Nutrition:

- Calories: 251
- Fat: 11 g
- Protein: 20 g
- Carbohydrates: 18.5 g

28. Blueberry Smoothie

Preparation time: 2 minutes

Cooking time: 0 minutes

Servings: 2

Ingredients:

- 2 cups fresh blueberries
- 1 cup ice
- 1/2 avocado ripe
- 1 tbsp whole chia seeds
- 1 tsp ground cinnamon
- 1/4 cup walnuts, preferably soaked overnight
- 1–2 collagen proteins coops or peptides (optional)
- 1/2 cup canned coconut milk (full fat)

- 1 1/2 cups water

Directions:

1. Mix all ingredients in a blender.
2. Blend it on high speed till creamy and smooth.

Nutrition:

- Calories: 315
- Fat: 18 g
- Protein: 11 g
- Carbohydrates: 61 g

29. Fried Egg and Greens

Preparation time: 12 minutes

Cooking time: 15 minutes

Servings: 1

Ingredients:

- 1/2 onion, diced
- 1 tbsp coconut oil
- 1 cup finely diced broccoli
- 2 cups chard and spinach each diced
- 1 tsp tamari
- 1 tsp avocado, sliced
- 1 egg
- 1/4 tsp red pepper flakes

Directions:

1. Cook onion in coconut oil for 5 minutes or until transparent. Add the broccoli and cook for another 5 minutes.
2. Stir in the chard, spinach, and tamari and simmer for 2 minutes, or until the greens have wilted.
3. Top with avocado and a fried egg, and red pepper flakes.

Nutrition:

- Calories: 387
- Fat: 7 g
- Protein: 6 g
- Carbohydrates: 0.4 g

30. Sweet Potato Pie Smoothie Bowl

Preparation time: 15 minutes

Cooking time: 3 minutes

Servings: 2

Ingredients:

- 1/4 cup large flake rolled oats
- 1/4 cup chopped unsalted pecans
- 2 tbsp pure maple syrup, divided
- 1 tsp coconut oil
- 2 cups frozen mango chunks
- 3/4 cup roasted, peeled and mashed sweet potato
- 1/2 cup canned coconut milk BPA-free
- 1 tsp pure vanilla extract
- 1/4 tsp nutmeg and cinnamon each ground

Directions:

1. Preheat the oven to 375°F. Use paper, like a small, rimmed baking sheet.
2. Combine oats, pecans, 1 tbsp maple syrup, and coconut oil in a small mixing bowl. Spread the mixture onto the prepared baking sheet and bake for 2 to 3 minutes, stirring once. Allow cooling fully before serving.
3. Blend mango, sweet potato, remaining 1 tbsp maple syrup, coconut milk, vanilla, nutmeg, and cinnamon in a high-powered blender until smooth.
4. Divide the mixture equally between two cold dishes and top with the oat mixture. Choose your favorite toppings to go on top.

Nutrition:

- Calories: 537
- Fat: 25 g
- Protein: 7 g
- Carbohydrates: 77 g

31. Cornmeal Pancakes With Black Bean Salsa and Cilantro Yogurt

Preparation time: 30 minutes

Cooking time: 10 minutes

Servings: 4

Ingredients:

Salsa:

- 1 (15 oz) unsalted black beans, BPA-free can drain and rinse
- 1 roma tomato, diced
- 1/4 cup diced red onion
- 1/4 cup chopped fresh cilantro
- 2 tbsp extra-virgin olive oil
- 1 tsp lime zest + 2 tbsp fresh lime juice
- 1/4 tsp chile powder each and sea salt

Yogurt:

- 1/2 cup whole-milk yogurt
- 3 tbsp chopped fresh cilantro
- 1/4 tsp sea salt
- 1/2 tsp ground black pepper

Pancakes:

- 1 cup almond flour
- 2/3 cup fine-ground cornmeal
- 1/4 cup coconut flour
- 1/4 cup arrowroot
- 2 tsp baking powder
- 1/2 tsp sea salt
- 2 large eggs
- 3/4 cup whole-milk buttermilk
- 1 jalapeño chile pepper, seeded and finely chopped
- Cooking spray

Directions:

1. Mix all the salsa ingredients in a medium mixing bowl.
2. Combine all yogurt ingredients in a small mixing dish.
3. Make pancakes: Mix almond flour, coconut flour, cornmeal, arrowroot, baking powder, and salt in a large mixing bowl. Mix the buttermilk and eggs together in a medium mixing bowl, then toss the dry ingredients until barely moistened. Add the jalapeño and fold it.
4. Spray a large nonstick pan along with cooking spray and place it over medium heat. Pour in 14 cups of batter for each pancake, working in batches. Cook for 2 minutes, or till bubbles appear on top; flip and cook for another 2 minutes, or until golden brown on the other side. Make a total of 8 pancakes by repeating the process.
5. Arrange pancakes on plates and serve with salsa and yogurt on the side.

Nutrition:

- Calories: 550
- Fat: 29 g
- Protein: 20 g
- Carbohydrates: 55 g

32. Southwestern-Style Black Bean Burritos

Preparation time: 25 minutes

Cooking time: 35 minutes

Servings: 4

Ingredients:

- 2 tbsp olive oil
- 1 yellow onion, small
- 1 (15 oz) pinto beans, BPA-free can drain and rinse
- 6 cups lightly packed baby spinach
- 1/4 tsp sea salt and black pepper, each divided
- 8 eggs, lightly beaten large
- 4 whole-grain tortillas large
- 1 cup jarred all-natural salsa or pico de gallo
- 3/4 cup shredded Monterey Jack or Mexican blend cheese

Directions:

1. Heat oil in a large nonstick pan over medium heat. Cook, occasionally turning, until onion is softened, approximately 6 minutes.
2. Add the beans, spinach, 1/8 tsp salt, and pepper, and simmer, often turning, for 4 to 5 minutes, or till the spinach is wilted. Allow cooling in a large mixing bowl.

3. Heat the remaining 1 tbsp oil in the same skillet over medium heat. Add the eggs and the remaining 1/8 tsp salt and pepper; cook, constantly stirring, for approximately 5 minutes, or till gently set. Cool in a separate big mixing bowl.
4. Spread a quarter of the bean mixture over the middle of each tortilla, leaving a 2-inch border on each side uncovered. Add a quarter of each egg, salsa, and cheese on the top.
5. Fold the tortilla's left and right sides over the contents. Roll firmly upward by lifting the bottom edge of the tortilla (the edge closest to you) over the contents. Wrap the burrito securely in a piece of foil sprayed with cooking spray, the oiled side facing the tortilla. Using the remaining tortillas and filling ingredients, repeat the process. (Tip: Store in the refrigerator for up to one day or freeze for up to one month.)
6. Heat oven or toaster oven to 375°F for heating. Arrange the burrito(s) on a baking sheet, foil-wrapped. Cook for 20 to 25 minutes, or until well cooked. Bake for 40 to 45 minutes if frozen.

Nutrition:

- Calories: 300
- Fat: 9 g
- Protein: 16 g
- Carbohydrates: 41 g

33. Fruit Yogurt Parfait

Preparation time: 2 minutes

Cooking time: 0 minutes

Servings: 1

Ingredients:

- 1 cup plain Greek yogurt
- 2 tbsp almonds and sunflower seeds each chopped
- 1 tbsp cacao nibs and maple syrup each

Directions:

1. Place Greek yogurt in a tall cup or dish and top it with almonds, cacao nibs, sunflower seeds, and maple syrup.

Nutrition:

- Calories: 379
- Fat: 9 g
- Protein: 11 g
- Carbohydrates: 67 g

34. Peanut Butter Maple Banana Muffins

Preparation time: 15 minutes

Cooking time: 25 minutes

Servings: 14

Ingredients:

- 2 cups oat flour
- 1 tsp baking powder
- 1/2 tsp baking soda
- 1/4 tsp coarse sea salt, optional
- 2 eggs large
- 2 tsp safflower oil
- 1/2 cup plus 2 tbsp greek yogurt, divided
- 1/4 cup pure maple syrup
- 1 tsp pure vanilla extract
- 3 bananas
- 2 tbsp natural unsalted crunchy peanut butter

Directions:

1. Preheat the oven to 350°F.
2. Prepare the batter as follows: Combine flour, baking powder, baking soda, and salt in a large mixing bowl (if using). 1/2 cup yogurt, maple syrup, and vanilla are whisked together in a small dish with 1 egg and oil. Stir the egg mixture into the flour mixture until it is barely incorporated. 1 banana, mashed and folded into the recipe until barely incorporated and no white streaks remain; the mixture should be lumpy.
3. Prepare the filling: Mash the remaining 2 bananas in a small bowl; whisk in the remaining 1 egg, 2 tbsp yogurt, and peanut butter until thoroughly incorporated.

4. Fill one-third of each muffin cup with batter after lining 14 cups with paper liners. Fill each with 1 tsp filling, then divide the remaining batter among the liners. Bake for 18 to 25 minutes, or until a toothpick inserted in the middle comes out clean. Allow 5 minutes for the muffins to cool in the pan before removing them to wire racks to cool completely.

Nutrition:

- Calories: 146
- Fat: 6 g
- Protein: 4 g
- Carbohydrates: 20 g

35. Ultimate Liver Detox Soup

Preparation time: 5 minutes

Cooking time: 20 minutes

Servings: 5

Ingredients:

- 2 tbsp extra-virgin olive oil
- 1 cup chopped shallot
- 1 tbsp grated ginger
- 2 garlic cloves, minced
- 4 cups homemade chicken broth
- 1 medium golden beet, diced
- 1 large carrot, sliced
- 1 cup shredded red cabbage
- 1 cup sliced mushrooms
- A handful pea pods, halved
- 1 hot chili pepper, sliced
- 1 cup chopped cauliflower
- 1 cup chopped broccoli
- 1 bell pepper, diced
- A pinch cayenne pepper
- A pinch sea salt
- 1 cup baby spinach
- 1 cup chopped kale
- 1 cup grape tomatoes, halved

Directions:

1. In a large skillet, heat olive oil until hot but not smoky; sauté in shallots, ginger, and garlic for about 2 minutes or until tender; stir in broth and bring the mixture to a gentle simmer.
2. Add in beets and carrots and simmer for about 5 minutes. Stir in hot pepper, cauliflower, and broccoli, and cook for about 3 minutes. stir in bell pepper, red cabbage, mushrooms, and peas, and cook for 1 minute.
3. Remove from heat and stir in salt and pepper. Stir in leafy greens and tomatoes and cover the pot for about 5 minutes. Serve.

Nutrition:

- Calories: 165
- Fat: 10 g
- Protein: 12 g
- Carbohydrates: 3 g

36. Pineapple, Matcha, and Beet Chia Pudding

Preparation time: 5 minutes

Cooking time: 10 minutes

Servings: 4

Ingredients:

- 1 cup chia seeds
- 1 tsp raw honey
- 2 cups almond milk
- 1 tsp matcha green tea powder
- 2 tbsp fresh beetroot juice
- 1 whole pineapple
- 1 cup freshly squeezed lemon juice
- 1 knob fresh ginger
- Toasted almonds and figs to serve

Directions:

1. Green Chia pudding layer: Add half chia seeds, raw honey, almond milk, and matcha green tea powder to the blender, and until very smooth; transfer to a bowl.
2. Beetroot layer: blend together beetroot and ginger with the remaining chia seeds, and lemon juice until very smooth; transfer to a separate bowl. In a food processor, puree the fresh pineapple until fine.

3. To assemble, layer the chia pudding in the bottom of the serving glasses, followed by the pureed pineapple and then the beetroot layer. Top with figs and toasted almonds for a crunchy finish.

Nutrition:

- Calories: 118
- Fat: 5 g
- Protein: 8 g
- Carbohydrates: g

37. Chicken Souvlaki

Preparation time: 5 minutes

Cooking time: 2 minutes

Servings: 4

Ingredients:

- 4 pieces (6-inch) pitas, cut into halves
- 2 cups roasted chicken breast skinless, boneless, and sliced
- 1/4 cup red onion, thinly sliced
- 1/2 tsp dried oregano
- 1/2 cup Greek yogurt, plain
- 1/2 cup plum tomato, chopped
- 1/2 cup cucumber, peeled, chopped
- 1/2 cup (2 oz) feta cheese, crumbled
- 1 tbsp olive oil, extra-virgin, divided
- 1 tbsp fresh dill, chopped
- 1 cup iceberg lettuce, shredded
- 1 1/4 tsp minced garlic, bottled, divided

Directions:

1. In a small mixing bowl, combine the yogurt, cheese, 1 tsp olive oil, and 1/4 tsp garlic until well mixed.
2. In a large skillet, heat the remaining olive oil over medium-high heat. Add the remaining 1 tsp garlic and the oregano; sauté for 20 seconds.
3. Add the chicken; cook for about 2 minutes or until the chicken is heated through. Add dill.
4. Put 1/4 cup chicken into each pita's halves. Top with 2 tbsp yogurt mix, 2 tbsp lettuce, 1 tbsp tomato, and 1 tbsp cucumber. Divide the onion between the pita halves.

Nutrition:

- Calories: 414
- Fat: 13.7 g (sat. fat: 6.4 g, poly. fat: 1.4 g, mono: 4.7 g)
- Protein: 32.3 g
- Carbohydrates: 38 g
- Fiber: 2 g
- Sodium: 595 mg
- Cholesterol: 81 mg

38. Overnight Superfood Parfait

Preparation time: 5 minutes

Cooking time: 10 minutes

Servings: 3

Ingredients:

- 1 cup almond milk
- 1 tsp spirulina powder
- 1 tsp raw honey
- 4 tbsp chia seeds
- 4 tbsp Greek yogurt, to serve
- 1 cup fresh cranberries, to serve
- 1 cup fresh blueberries
- 1 cup toasted almonds

Directions:

1. In a bowl, mix together all the ingredients until well combined; let set overnight. To serve, add half of the yogurt to a serving glass and top with a third of berries and toasted almonds; repeat the layers until the glass is full. Enjoy!

Nutrition:

- Calories: 242
- Fat: 19 g
- Protein: 12 g
- Carbohydrates: 7 g

39. Onion Omelet

Preparation time: 5 minutes

Cooking time: 10 minutes

Servings: 2

Ingredients:

- 4 eggs
- 1/2 tsp salt
- 1/2 tsp black pepper
- 2 tbsp olive oil
- 1/2 cup cheese
- 1/2 tsp basil
- 2 cups red onion

Directions:

In a bowl, whisk together the eggs, salt, black pepper, cheese, and basil until well combined.
Heat the olive oil in a skillet over medium heat. Add the onions and cook until they are soft and translucent, about 5 minutes.
Pour the egg mixture over the onions and cook for 2 to 3 minutes per side or until the omelet is cooked through.
Slide the omelet onto a plate and serve.

Nutrition:

- Calories: 320
- Fat: 22 g
- Protein: 20 g
- Carbohydrates: 25 g

40. Stuffed Figs

Preparation time: 5 minutes

Cooking time: 15 minutes

Servings: 2

Ingredients:

- 7 oz fresh figs
- 1 tbsp cream cheese
- 1/2 tsp walnuts, chopped
- 4 bacon slices
- 1/4 tsp paprika
- 1/4 tsp salt
- 1/2 tsp canola oil
- 1/2 tsp honey

Directions:

1. Make the crosswise cuts in every fig.
2. In the shallow bowl mix up together cream cheese, walnuts, paprika, and salt.
3. Fill the figs with cream cheese mixture and wrap them in the bacon.
4. Secure the fruits with toothpicks and sprinkle them with honey.
5. Line the baking tray with baking paper.
6. Place the preparation of the figs in the tray and sprinkle them with canola oil gently.
7. Bake the figs for 15 minutes at 350°F.

Nutrition:

- Calories: 299
- Fat: 19.4 g
- Protein: 15.2 g
- Carbohydrates: 16.7 g
- Fiber: 2.3 g

41. Superfood Liver Cleansing Soup

Preparation time: 5 minutes

Cooking time: 20 minutes

Servings: 3

Ingredients:

- 1/4 cup water
- 2 garlic cloves, minced
- 1/2 red onion, diced
- 1 tbsp fresh ginger, peeled and minced
- 1 cup chopped tomatoes
- 1 small head of broccoli, florets
- 3 medium carrots, diced
- 3 celery stalks, diced
- 6 cups water
- 1/4 tsp cinnamon
- 1 tsp turmeric

- 1/8 tsp cayenne pepper
- Freshly ground black pepper to taste
- Juice of 1 lemon
- 1 cup purple cabbage, chopped
- 2 cups kale, torn into pieces

Directions:

1. Bring a large pot of water to a gentle boil over medium heat. Add garlic and onion and cook for about 2 minutes, stirring occasionally.
2. Stir in carrots, broccoli, tomatoes, fresh ginger, and celery, and cook for another 3 minutes. Stir in cayenne, turmeric, cinnamon, and black pepper.
3. Add half a cup of water to the pot and bring to a gentle boil; lower heat and simmer until the veggies and tender, for about 15 minutes.
4. Stir in kale, cabbage, and fresh lemon juice during the last 2 minutes of cooking. Serve hot or warm.

Nutrition:

- Calories: 283.6
- Fat: 31 g
- Protein: 10.9 g
- Carbohydrates: 31 g

42. Asparagus With Egg

Preparation time: 5 minutes

Cooking time: 20 minutes

Servings: 4

Ingredients:

- 1 lb asparagus
- 4–5 pieces prosciutto
- 1/4 tsp salt
- 2 eggs

Directions:

1. Trim the asparagus and season with salt.
2. Wrap each asparagus piece with prosciutto.
3. Place the wrapped asparagus in a baking dish.
4. Bake at 375°F for 22 to 25 minutes.
5. When ready remove from the oven and serve.

Nutrition:

- Calories: 460
- Fat: 30 g
- Protein: 20 g
- Carbohydrates: 35 g

43. Vanilla Oats

Preparation time: 5 minutes

Cooking time: 10 minutes

Servings: 4

Ingredients:

- 1/2 cup rolled oats
- 1 cup milk
- 1 tsp vanilla extract
- 1 tsp ground cinnamon
- 2 tsp honey
- 2 tbsp Plain yogurt
- 1 tsp butter

Directions:

1. Pour milk into the saucepan and bring it to a boil.
2. Add rolled oats and stir well.
3. Close the lid and simmer the oats for 5 minutes over medium heat. The cooked oats will absorb all milk.
4. Then add butter and stir the oats well.
5. In the separated bowl, whisk together Plain yogurt with honey, cinnamon, and vanilla extract.
6. Transfer the cooked oats to the serving bowls.
7. Top the oats with the yogurt mixture.

Nutrition:

- Calories: 243
- Fat: 20.2 g
- Protein: 13.3 g
- Carbohydrates: 2.8 g

- Fiber: 1 g

44. Carrot Omelet

Preparation time: 15 minutes

Cooking time: 20 minutes

Servings: 4

Ingredients:

- 2 eggs
- 1/4 tsp salt
- 1/4 tsp black pepper
- 1 tbsp olive oil
- 1/4 cup cheese
- 1/4 tsp basil
- 1 cup carrot

Directions:

1. In a bowl combine all ingredients together and mix well.
2. In a skillet heat olive oil and pour the egg mixture.
3. Cook for 1 to 2 minutes per side.
4. When ready remove the omelet from the skillet and serve.

Nutrition:

- Calories: 320
- Fat: 11 g
- Protein: 10 g
- Carbohydrates: 50 g

45. Veggie Omelet

Preparation time: 5 minutes

Cooking time: 20 minutes

Servings: 3

Ingredients:

- 3 egg whites
- 1 egg
- 1/2 tsp extra-virgin olive oil
- 1/8 tsp red pepper flakes
- 1/8 tsp ground nutmeg
- 1/8 tsp garlic powder
- A pinch of salt
- 1/8 tsp ground black pepper
- 1/2 cup sliced fresh mushrooms
- 2 tbsp chopped red bell pepper
- 1/4 cup chopped green onion
- 1/2 cup chopped tomato
- 1 cup chopped fresh spinach

Directions:

1. In a large bowl, whisk together egg whites, egg, garlic powder, red pepper flakes, nutmeg, salt, and pepper until well blended.
2. Heat olive oil in a skillet over medium heat; add green onion, mushrooms, and bell pepper and cook for about 5 minutes or until tender; stir in tomato and egg mixture and cook for about 5 minutes per side or until egg is set. Slice and serve hot with spinach.

Nutrition:

- Calories: 283.6
- Fat: 11.5 g
- Protein: 10.9 g
- Carbohydrates: 31 g

46. Beets Omelet

Preparation time: 5 minutes

Cooking time: 10 minutes

Servings: 1

Ingredients:

- 2 eggs
- 1/4 tsp salt
- 1/4 tsp black pepper
- 1 tbsp olive oil
- 1/4 cup cheese
- 1/4 tsp basil
- 1 cup beets

Directions:

1. In a bowl combine all ingredients together and mix well.
2. In a skillet heat olive oil and pour the egg mixture.
3. Cook for 1 to 2 minutes per side.
4. When ready remove the omelet from the skillet and serve.

Nutrition:

- Calories: 320
- Fat: 11 g
- Protein: 10 g
- Carbohydrates: 50 g

47. Spiced French Toast

Preparation time: 5 minutes

Cooking time: 12 minutes

Servings: 4

Ingredients:

- 4 eggs
- 1/2 cup Homemade Rice Milk (or use unsweetened store-bought or almond milk)
- 1/4 cup freshly squeezed orange juice
- 1 tsp ground cinnamon
- 1/2 tsp ground ginger
- A pinch ground cloves
- 1 tbsp unsalted butter, divided
- 8 slices of white bread

Directions:

1. Whisk eggs, rice milk, orange juice, cinnamon, ginger, and cloves until well blended in a large bowl.
2. Melt half the butter in a large skillet. It should be in medium-high heat only.
3. Dredge four of the bread slices in the egg mixture until well soaked, and place them in the skillet.
4. Cook the toast until golden brown on both sides, turning once, about 6 minutes total.
5. Repeat with the remaining butter and bread.
6. Serve 2 pieces of hot French toast to each person.

Nutrition:

- Calories: 236
- Fat: 11 g
- Saturated fat: 4 g
- Protein: 11 g
- Carbohydrates: 27 g
- Fiber: 1 g
- Sodium: 84 mg
- Cholesterol: 220 mg
- Phosphorus: 119 mg
- Potassium: 158 mg

Chapter 10. Lunch Recipes

48. Mixed Veggies and Grapefruit Salad With Dijon Grapefruit Vinaigrette

Preparation time: 20 minutes

Cooking time: 0 minutes

Servings: 5

Ingredients:

- 8 cups chopped kale (no stems)
- 1/2 grapefruit, peeled and segmented
- 1 avocado, chopped
- 2 tbsp sliced almonds

Dijon Grapefruit Vinaigrette:

- 1 tsp finely chopped shallot
- 2 tbsp extra-virgin olive oil
- 3 tbsp fresh grapefruit juice
- 1/2 tsp Dijon mustard
- Sea salt to taste
- Freshly ground pepper, to taste

Directions:

1. To make the Dijon grapefruit vinaigrette, in a food processor bowl, grapefruit juice, Dijon mustard, oil, shallot, salt, and pepper to taste, and process until smooth.
2. In a large mixing bowl, place the kale together with the vinaigrette and massage well with your hands. Transfer to a plate and let it slightly soften for about 10 minutes.
3. Arrange the grapefruit segment and chopped avocado over the kale and sprinkle with almonds. Serve right away.

Nutrition:

- Calories: 71
- Fat: 5.7 g
- Protein: 2.3 g
- Carbohydrates: 4.2 g
- Fiber: 0 g
- Sugar: 0.8 g
- Sodium: 42.3 mg
- Potassium: 0 mg

49. Quick Hummus and Greek Salad

Preparation time: 10 minutes

Cooking time: 0 minutes

Servings: 1

Ingredients:

- 1/3 cup cherry tomatoes, halved
- 1/3 cup sliced cucumber
- 2 cups arugula
- 1 tbsp chopped red onion
- 1 1/2 tbsp extra-virgin olive oil
- 2 tsp red wine vinegar
- 1/8 tsp freshly ground black pepper

- 1 tbsp feta cheese
- 1 4-inch whole-wheat pita
- 1/4 cup hummus

Directions:

1. Combine the cucumber, onion, vinegar, tomatoes, oil, arugula, and pepper on a serving plate and toss.
2. Top mixture with feta and serve with hummus and pita. Enjoy!

Nutrition:

- Calories: 422
- Fat: 29.9 g
- Protein: 10.9 g
- Carbohydrates: 4.9 g
- Fiber: 7.3 g
- Sugar: 4.3 g
- Sodium: 485.8 mg
- Potassium: 543.8 mg

50. Quick Pesto Chicken Salad With Greens

Preparation time: 10 minutes

Cooking time: 20 minutes

Servings: 4

Ingredients:

- 1 lb boneless, skinless chicken breast, trimmed
- 1/4 cup pesto
- 1/4 cup low-fat mayonnaise
- 3 tbsp finely chopped red onion
- 2 tbsp red wine vinegar
- 8 cups mixed salad greens
- 2 tbsp extra-virgin olive oil
- 1-pint grape or cherry tomatoes halved
- 1/4 tsp sea salt
- 1/4 tsp ground pepper

Directions:

1. In a saucepan over medium heat, place the chicken, pour in water, and let the water cover the chicken by 1 inch.
2. Cover the saucepan and let it boil over medium-high heat.
3. Reduce the heat to low heat and let it simmer for 15 minutes, or until the chicken is no longer pink in the center.
4. Transfer chicken to a chopping board to cool and shred into small-small pieces.
5. In a medium mixing bowl. Combine the pesto, onion, and mayonnaise. Add shreds of chicken and toss until coated.
6. In a large mixing bowl, combine the vinegar, oil, salt, and pepper and whisk well. Add the tomatoes and greens and toss to coat.
7. Divide the salad equally among 4 serving plates and top with chicken salad. Enjoy!

Nutrition:

- Calories: 324
- Fat: 19.7 g
- Protein: 27.1 g
- Carbohydrates: 9.2 g
- Fiber: 2.3 g
- Sugar: 3.2 g
- Sodium: 453.9 mg
- Potassium: 542.2 mg

51. Crispy Tofu With Vegetable Salad

Preparation time: 10 minutes

Cooking time: 20 minutes

Servings: 2

Ingredients:

- 8 oz package of extra-firm water-packed tofu, cut tofu crosswise into 4 equal pieces, and press for 3 hours
- 3 tbsp extra-virgin olive oil, divided
- 1 tbsp chopped fresh basil
- 1 tsp chopped fresh oregano
- 2 tbsp lemon juice
- 1 egg large
- 2 tbsp all-purpose flour
- 1/3 cup grated Parmesan cheese
- 1/6 cup whole-wheat panko breadcrumbs
- 1/16 tsp sea salt
- 1/2 tsp freshly ground black pepper

For salad:

- 2 ripe medium-sized tomatoes cut each one of them into 6 wedges
- 1 cup thinly sliced sweet onion
- 1/4 cup Castelvetrano olives
- 2 tbsp chopped fresh oregano, divided
- 1 1/2 tbsp extra-virgin olive oil
- 2 tbsp chopped fresh basil, divided
- 1 tbsp red wine vinegar
- 1/2 tbsp lemon juice
- 1/8 tsp freshly ground black pepper
- 1/16 tsp sea salt

Directions:

Combine 1 tbsp oil, 1 tsp oregano, 2 tbsp of lemon juice, 1 tbsp basil, 1/2 tsp pepper, and 1/16 tsp salt on a baking sheet.
Add the pressed tofu and mix until well coated, cover, and put in the fridge for 2 hours or more, turn often.
Combine the olives, tomatoes, onion, and oil, 1 tbsp basil, 1/2 tsp oregano, lemon juice, vinegar, pepper, and salt in a large mixing bowl, and toss well. Put salad aside, tossing occasionally.
Remove the tofu from the marinade, pat dry, and discard the marinade. Place flour in a shallow bowl.
Crack the egg in a shallow bowl and lightly beat. Combine the panko and parmesan in another shallow bowl.
Dip the tofu in the flour bowl, shake off any excess, dip in the egg bowl and shake off any excess, and then in the panko and parmesan mixture and press well to coat.
In a nonstick skillet over medium heat, heat 1 tbsp oil until shimmering and add 1/2 of the tofu.
Lower the heat to low heat and cook for 4 minutes on each side or until browned, turning once.
Transfer to a plate lined with a paper towel and then repeat the process with the remaining 1 tbsp oil and tofu.
Divide the salad among 2 serving bowls and top with tofu and the remaining 1/2 tsp oregano and 1 tbsp basil. Enjoy!

Nutrition:

- Calories: 275
- Fat: 21.9 g
- Protein: 8.8 g
- Carbohydrates: 11.5 g
- Fiber: 2.5 g
- Sugar: 3.4 g
- Sodium: 320.7 mg
- Potassium: 293.4 mg

52. Healthy Spinach Salad

Preparation time: 20 minutes

Cooking time: 60 minutes

Servings: 8

Ingredients:

- 1 large Chioggia beet
- 1/4 cup finely chopped green garlic, white part mostly
- 1 cup whole-milk plain Greek yogurt
- 1/3 cup chopped fresh mint
- 4 tbsp extra-virgin olive oil, divided
- 2 tbsp finely chopped scallion
- 1 tsp dried oregano
- 1 lb mature spinach, finely sliced
- 1 tbsp butter, melted
- 1 tsp dried mint
- 1 tsp ground Aleppo
- 1 tsp sea salt
- 1/2 tsp ground pepper

Directions:

1. Place the beet in a saucepan, cover with water by 1 inch and bring to a boil over high heat, cook for about 50 minutes or until tender. Remove from heat and transfer to a chopping board and let it cool off. Peel and julienne the beet, when it is cooled.
2. In a small saucepan over medium-low heat, heat 2 tbsp oil together with green garlic and cook for about 6 minutes or until garlic is softened but not brown.
3. Remove from heat and transfer to a large mixing bowl. Add the remaining 2 tbsp oil, fresh mint, yogurt, scallion, salt, and pepper to the bowl and whisk well.
4. Add the beet to the bowl together with the spinach, add the dressing and toss to coat.

5. Divide among 8 serving plates. Drizzle each plate with butter and sprinkle oregano, dried mint, and Aleppo.

Note: you can cook the beet ahead of time and save it in the fridge for up to 3 days.

Nutrition:

- Calories: 147
- Fat: 11.7 g
- Protein: 4.4 g
- Carbohydrates: 7.6 g
- Fiber: 2.9 g
- Sugar: 3.8 g
- Sodium: 479 mg
- Potassium: 479.2 mg

53. Roasted Chicken and Mushrooms Salad

Preparation time: 40 minutes

Cooking time: 20 minutes

Servings: 4

Ingredients:

- 3 garlic cloves, minced
- 5 tbsp extra-virgin olive oil
- 3 tsp fennel seeds, crushed, divided
- 1/2 tsp ground pepper, divided
- 10 oz mushrooms, quartered
- 1 lb chicken tenders halved crosswise
- 4 medium carrots, sliced 1/2 inch thick
- 1 medium onion, cut into 3/4-inch wedges
- 1 1/2 cups water
- 1 cup quinoa
- 3 tbsp sherry vinegar or red wine vinegar
- 8 cups torn escarole
- 1 tsp sea salt, divided

Directions:

1. Preheat the oven to 475°F.
2. On a small plate, place the garlic together with 3/4 tsp salt and mash with a knife. Transfer the mashed garlic to a large mixing bowl and add oil, 2 tsp fennel seeds, and 1/4 tsp pepper and whisk well.
3. In a medium bowl, carrots, mushrooms, and onion, drizzle 2 tbsp oil mixture and toss well to coat.
4. Spread the veggies on a large-rimmed baking dish and roast for about 10 minutes.
5. While the veggies are cooking, Place the quinoa in a saucepan, add water and let it boil over medium-high heat.
6. Reduce the heat to low heat and let it simmer for 10 minutes. Remove quinoa from heat, cover it, and let it stand for about 5 minutes.
7. Place the chicken in a medium bowl and add the oil mixture, 2 tsp oil, 1 tsp fennel seeds, 1/4 tsp salt, and 1/4 tsp pepper, and toss until coated.
8. Add the veggies, stir and nestle the chicken among the veggies and continue to roast for more than 10 minutes or until the chicken is cooked through.
9. Add vinegar to the remaining oil mixture and whisk well. Add escarole and quinoa to the mixture and toss well with a dressing
10. To serve, top with the roasted veggies with chicken. Enjoy!

Nutrition:

- Calories: 516
- Fat: 23.6 g
- Protein: 33.6 g
- Carbohydrates: 43 g
- Fiber: 9.7 g
- Sugar: 7.8 g
- Sodium: 711.2 mg
- Potassium: 1242 mg

54. Chickpea, Broccoli, and Pomegranate Salad

Preparation time: 10 minutes

Cooking time: 0 minutes

Servings: 6

Ingredients:

- 1/4 cup finely sliced red onion
- 1/3 tsp ground cumin

- 1 cup whole-milk plain yogurt
- 2 tbsp tahini
- 2 tbsp extra-virgin olive oil
- 1 tbsp lemon juice
- 4 cups bite-size broccoli florets
- 1 can low-sodium chickpeas, rinsed cup pomegranate seeds
- 1 tsp salt, divided
- 1. tsp freshly ground black pepper

Directions:

1. Pour water into a small bowl, add the onion and soak for 10 minutes, and drain.
2. In a small dry skillet over medium heat, place the cumin and toast, stir for 2 minutes or until fragrant
3. Remove from heat and transfer to a large mixing bowl, add lemon juice, tahini, oil, yogurt, 1/2 tsp salt, and pepper, and whisk until well mixed.
4. Add chickpeas, broccoli, pomegranate seeds, and onion to the bowl toss until well combined, and let it stand for at least 10 minutes.
5. Season with the remaining 1/4 tsp salt and toss well. Enjoy!

Nutrition:

- Calories: 162
- Fat: 8.8 g
- Protein: 6.2 g
- Carbohydrates: 16.1 g
- Fiber: 4.3 g
- Sugar: 3.6 g
- Sodium: 344.2 mg
- Potassium: 368.8 mg

55. Anchovy, Orange, and Olive Salad

Preparation time: 30 minutes

Cooking time: 0 minutes

Servings: 4

Ingredients:

- 1 small red onion, finely slice in a round shape
- 16 black olives pitted and halved
- 4 small blood oranges
- 3 tbsp extra-virgin olive oil
- 6 anchovy fillets
- 1 tbsp fresh lemon juice
- 1/8 tsp freshly ground black pepper

Directions:

1. With a paring knife, peel the oranges and cut off the white pith and the membrane that covers the orange on the aside.
2. Place the orange on a plate and slice it into a round shape, making the round shape as thin as possible.
3. Assemble the sliced orange on a serving plate, and keep the juice aside. Add the onion all over the orange slices and top with olives followed by the anchovy fillets.
4. Add the lemon and orange juice over the mixture, drizzle oil and then sprinkle with black pepper.
5. Keep the salad for 30 minutes to stand at room temperature before serving.

Nutrition:

- Calories: 202
- Fat: 15.2 g
- Protein: 3.1 g
- Carbohydrates: 14.6 g
- Fiber: 2.8 g
- Sugar: 9.8 g
- Sodium: 465. 3 mg
- Potassium: 236.8 mg

56. Vegetable and Chickpea Salad

Preparation time: 20 minutes

Cooking time: 20 minutes

Servings: 6

Ingredients:

- 1 large eggplant, thinly sliced (slice into1/4 inch in thickness)
- Salt to taste
- 5 tbsp extra virgin olive oil
- 3 Roma tomatoes, diced

- 1 cup cooked or canned chickpeas, drained
- 3 tbsp Za'atar spice, divided
- 1/2 English cucumber, diced
- 1 cup chopped dill
- 1 small red onion, sliced into a round shape
- 1 cup chopped parsley

For the Garlic Vinaigrette:

- 1 lime juice
- 1–2 garlic cloves, minced
- 1/3 cup extra virgin olive oil
- Sea salt to taste
- Freshly ground black pepper to taste

Directions:

1. Place the eggplant on a tray and sprinkle it with salt as needed. Set aside and let sit for 30 minutes.
2. Line a baking sheet with a paper bag topped with a paper towel and place it closer to a stove. Dries the eggplant.
3. Heat 5 tbsp oil in a skillet over medium-high heat until heated, add the eggplant and cook 5 minutes turn and cook another 5 minutes or golden brown turn.
4. Remove from heat with a slotted spatula and repeat the process until no more eggplant, don't overcrowd the eggplant in the pan.
5. Arrange the eggplant on a tray lined with a paper towel to drain.
6. When you are done frying, arrange the cooled eggplant on a serving plate and sprinkle with 1 tbsp Za'atar.
7. In a medium bowl, combine the cucumbers, tomatoes, red onions, chickpeas, dill, and parsley; add the remaining 2 tbsp Za'atar, and mix.
8. In a small mixing bowl, combine the garlic, lime juice, oil, salt, and pepper to taste and whisk well.
9. Drizzle the fried eggplant with 2 tbsp. of the dressing and then pour the rest of the dressing into the chickpea salad and mix well.
10. To serve, combine the eggplant and the chickpea on a serving plate and serve.

Nutrition:

- Calories: 380
- Fat: 15.3 g
- Protein: 11.1 g
- Carbohydrates: 17.3 g
- Fiber: 9.6 g
- Sugar: 5.3 g
- Sodium: 435.5 mg
- Potassium: 0 mg

57. Tabouli With Veggies Salad

Preparation time: 20 minutes

Cooking time: 0 minutes

Servings: 7

Ingredients:

- 1/2 cup extra-fine bulgur wheat, washed
- 1 English cucumber, very finely chopped
- 2 bunches of parsley, remove part of the stems, washed, dried, and finely chopped
- 4 firm Roma tomatoes, very finely chopped
- 4 green onions, white and green parts, finely chopped
- 12–15 fresh mint leaves, remove the stems, washed, dry, and finely chopped
- Sea salt to taste
- 4 tbsp lime juice
- 4 tbsp Early Harvest extra virgin olive oil

Directions:

1. Soak the bulgur in filtered water for 7 minutes, drain and squeeze out all the liquid in it and set aside.
2. Combine the herbs, vegetables, and green onions in a large mixing bowl, add the bulgur, and season to taste with salt and mix well.
3. Add the oil and lime and mix well. Cover the bowl and put it in the fridge for about 30 minutes. Remove from fridge and divide among 7 plates and enjoy!

Nutrition:

- Calories: 190
- Fat: 10 g
- Protein: 3.2 g
- Carbohydrates: 25 g

- Fiber: 3.1 g
- Sugar: 5.3 g
- Sodium: 435.5 mg
- Potassium: 0 mg

58. Healthy Fattoush Salad

Preparation time: 20 minutes

Cooking time: 0 minutes

Servings: 6

Ingredients:

- 2 loaves of pita bread
- Extra virgin olive oil to taste
- 1/2 tsp sumac
- Sea salt to taste
- Freshly ground black pepper to taste
- 1 heart of Romaine lettuce, chopped
- 1 cucumber, chopped
- 4 Roma tomatoes, chopped
- 4 green onions chopped
- 5 radishes, stems removed and thinly sliced
- 2 cups chopped fresh parsley leaves, remove the stems
- 1 cup chopped fresh mint leaves

For the lime-vinaigrette:

- 1 1/2 lime juice
- 1 tsp ground sumac
- 1/3 cup extra virgin olive oil
- 1/4 tsp ground cinnamon scant
- 1/4 tsp ground allspice
- Sea salt to taste
- Freshly ground black pepper to taste

Directions:

1. Place the pita bread in a toaster oven and toast until crunchy but not brown.
2. Heat 3 tbsp oil in a large saucepan; break the pita bread into pieces and add to the oil. Fry the pita bread for 5 minutes, or until brown, tossing often as you cook.
3. Add 1/2 tsp sumac, salt, and pepper to the saucepan. Remove from heat and transfer to a paper towel to drain.
4. Combine the cucumber, lettuce, green onions, and tomatoes in a large bowl together with the mint, parsley, and slice radish.
5. Combine the lime juice, oil, lemon, and spices in a small bowl and whisk well.
6. Add the dress to the salad and toss gently, top with the pita chips and toss again. Enjoy!

Nutrition:

- Calories: 345
- Fat: 20.4 g
- Protein: 9.1 g
- Carbohydrates: 39.8 g
- Fiber: 0 g
- Sugar: 11.4 gFat: 20.4 g
- Sodium: 177.6 mg
- Potassium: 0 mg

59. Veggies With Chickpea Salad

Preparation time: 15 minutes

Cooking time: 0 minutes

Servings: 7

Ingredients:

- 3 1/2 cups cooked chickpeas, drained and well rinsed
- 1/2 green bell pepper, cored and finely chopped
- 2 1/2 cups cherry tomatoes, sliced in halves
- 3–5 green onions finely chopped
- 1/2 cup sun-dried tomatoes, one preserved in jars with olive oil is better
- 1/3 cup pitted Kalamata olives
- 1/2 cup freshly chopped mint or basil leaves
- 1/4 cup pitted green olives
- 1/2 cup freshly chopped parsley leaves

For dressing:

- 1/4 cup extra virgin olive oil
- 1 garlic clove, minced
- 2 tbsp white wine vinegar
- 2 tbsp lemon juice
- 1 tsp ground sumac
- 1/2 tsp Aleppo pepper
- Sea salt to taste

- Freshly ground black pepper to taste

Directions:

1. Combine the chickpeas, veggies, sun-dried tomatoes, olives, and fresh herbs in a large mixing bowl and mix well.
2. Combine the oil, lemon juice, vinegar, garlic, spices, salt, and pepper to taste in a small mixing bowl and mix well.
3. Add the dressing to the salad and gently mix until coated. Cover the salad bowl with a lid and put it in the fridge for at least 30 minutes before serving.
4. Remove the salad from the fridge, give it a quick stir, taste and make some necessary adjustments if possible. Enjoy!

Nutrition:

- Calories: 267
- Fat: 7.6 g
- Protein: 12.4 g
- Carbohydrates: 39.5 g
- Fiber: 0 g
- Sugar: 8.1 g
- Sodium: 17.6 mg
- Potassium: 0 mg

60. Cheesy Scrambled Eggs With Fresh Herbs

Preparation time: 5 minutes

Cooking time: 10 minutes

Servings: 4

Ingredients:

- 3 eggs
- 2 egg whites
- 1/2 cup cream cheese
- 1/4 cup unsweetened rice milk
- 1 tbsp chopped scallion green part only
- 1 tbsp chopped fresh tarragon
- 2 tbsp unsalted butter
- Ground black pepper to taste

Directions:

1. In a container, mix the eggs, rice milk, egg whites, scallions, cream cheese, and tarragon until mixed and smooth.
2. Melt the butter in a skillet.
3. Pour in the egg mix and cook, stirring, for 5 minutes or until the eggs are thick and curds creamy.
4. Season with pepper and serve.

Nutrition:

- Calories: 221
- Fat: 19 g
- Protein: 8 g
- Carbohydrates: 3 g
- Sodium: 193 mg
- Phosphorus: 119 mg
- Potassium: 140 mg

61. Couscous With Artichokes, Sun-Dried Tomatoes, and Feta

Preparation time: 5 minutes

Cooking time: 8 minutes

Servings: 4

Ingredients:

- 3 cups chicken breast, cooked, chopped
- 2 1/3 cups water, divided
- 2 jars (6 oz each) of marinated artichoke hearts, undrained
- 1/4 tsp black pepper, freshly ground
- 1/2 cup tomatoes, sun-dried
- 1/2 cup (2 oz) feta cheese, crumbled
- 1 cup flat-leaf parsley, fresh, chopped
- 1 3/4 cups whole-wheat Israeli couscous, uncooked
- 1 can (14 1/2 oz) vegetable broth

Directions:

1. In a microwavable bowl, combine 2 cups of the water and the tomatoes. Microwave on HIGH for about 3 minutes or until the water boils. When water is boiling, remove from the microwave, cover, and let stand for about 3

minutes or until the tomatoes are soft; drain, chop, and set aside.
2. In a large saucepan, place the vegetable broth and the remaining 1/3 cup of water; bring to a boil. Stir in the couscous, cover, reduce heat, and simmer for about 8 minutes or until tender. Remove the pan from the heat; add the tomatoes and the remaining ingredients. Stir to combine.

Nutrition:

- Calories: 419
- Fat: 14.1 g (sat. fat: 3.9 g, poly. fat: 0.8 g, mono: 1.4 g)
- Protein: 30.2 g
- Carbohydrates: 42.5 g
- Fiber: 2.6 g
- Sodium: 677 mg
- Cholesterol: 64 mg

62. Lemon Muffins

Preparation time: 5 minutes

Cooking time: 30 minutes

Servings: 2 muffins

Ingredients:

- 1 egg
- 1/2 tbsp olive oil
- 1/2 cup milk
- 1 cup whole wheat flour
- 1/2 tsp baking soda
- 1/8 tsp baking powder
- 1/2 tsp cinnamon
- 1/2 cup lemon slices

Directions:

In a bowl, whisk together the egg, olive oil, and milk.
In another bowl, mix together the flour, baking soda, baking powder, and cinnamon.
Combine the wet and dry ingredients and mix well.
Divide the batter among 4 muffin cups, filling each one 2/3 full.

Bake at 375°F for 18 to 20 minutes or until a toothpick inserted into the center of a muffin comes out clean. Remove from the oven and let cool before serving.

Nutrition:

- Calories: 150
- Fat: 3 g
- Protein: 5 g
- Carbohydrates: 26 g

63. Citrus Chicken With Delicious Cold Soup

Preparation time: 5 minutes

Cooking time: 30 minutes

Servings: 3

Ingredients:

- 2 tbsp extra-virgin olive oil
- 500 g chicken breast
- 1 tsp fresh rosemary
- 1 lemon, sliced
- 1 orange, sliced

For the cold soup:

- 2 tbsp apple cider vinegar
- 1/4 cup green pepper, chopped
- 1/4 cup cucumber, chopped
- 1/2 cup onion, chopped
- 3 garlic cloves, minced
- 1 cup stewed tomatoes

Directions:

1. Generously coat chicken with extra virgin olive oil and cover with rosemary, lemon, and orange slices. Bake in the oven at 350°F for about 30 minutes.
2. In a blender, blend together all the soup ingredients until very smooth, and then serve with chicken and cooked brown rice.

Nutrition:

- Calories: 165
- Fat: 10 g
- Protein: 12 g
- Carbohydrates: 3 g

64. Eggs and Veggies

Preparation time: 5 minutes

Cooking time: 10 minutes

Servings: 4

Ingredients:

- 2 tomatoes, chopped
- 2 eggs, beaten
- 1 bell pepper, chopped
- 1 tsp tomato paste
- 1/4 cup water
- 1 tsp butter
- 1/2 white onion, diced
- 1/2 tsp chili flakes
- 1/3 tsp sea salt

Directions:

1. Put butter in the pan and melt it.
2. Add bell pepper and cook it for 3 minutes over medium heat. Stir it from time to time.
3. After this, add diced onion and cook it for 2 minutes more.
4. Stir the vegetables and add tomatoes.
5. Cook them for 5 minutes over medium-low heat.
6. Then add water and tomato paste. Stir well.
7. Add beaten eggs, chili flakes, and sea salt.
8. Stir well and cook for 4 minutes over the medium-low heat.
9. The cooked meal should be half runny.

Nutrition:

- Calories: 67
- Fat: 3.4 g
- Protein: 3.8 g
- Carbohydrates: 6.4 g
- Fiber: 1.5 g

65. Toxin Flush and Detox Salad

Preparation time: 5 minutes

Cooking time: 10 minutes

Servings: 3

Ingredients:

For the salad:

- 2 cups broccoli florets
- 2 cups red cabbage, thinly sliced
- 2 cups chopped kale
- 1 cup grated carrot
- 1 red bell pepper, sliced into strips
- 2 avocados, diced
- 1/2 cup chopped parsley
- 1 cup walnuts
- 1 tbsp sesame seeds

For the dressing:

- 2 tsp gluten-free mustard
- 1 tbsp freshly grated ginger
- 1/2 cup fresh lemon juice
- 1/3 cup grapeseed oil
- 1 tsp raw honey
- 1/4 tsp salt

Directions:

1. In a blender, blend all the dressing ingredients until well blended; set aside.
2. In a salad bowl, mix broccoli, carrots, kale, cabbage, and bell pepper; add the dressing to the salad and mix until the salad is evenly coated.
3. Add diced avocado, parsley, walnuts, and sesame seed; toss again to coat and serve.

Nutrition:

- Calories: 283.6
- Fat: 11.5 g
- Protein: 10.9 g
- Carbohydrates: 31 g

66. Olive and Milk Bread

Preparation time: 5 minutes

Cooking time: 50 minutes

Servings: 6

Ingredients:

- 1 cup black olives, pitted, chopped
- 1 tbsp olive oil
- 1/2 tsp fresh yeast
- 1/2 cup milk, preheated
- 1/2 tsp salt
- 1 tsp baking powder
- 2 cup wheat flour, whole grain
- 2 eggs, beaten
- 1 tsp butter, melted
- 1 tsp sugar

Directions:

1. In the big bowl combine together fresh yeast, sugar, and milk. Stir it until the yeast is dissolved.
2. Then add salt, baking powder, butter, olive oil, and eggs. Stir the dough mixture until homogenous and add 1 cup of wheat flour. Mix it up until smooth.
3. Add olives and remaining flour. Knead the non-sticky dough.
4. Transfer the dough to the non-sticky dough mold.
5. Bake the bread for 50 minutes at 350°F.
6. Check if the bread is cooked with the help of a toothpick. If it is dry, the bread is cooked.
7. Remove the bread from the oven and let it chill for 10 to 15 minutes.
8. Remove it from the loaf mold and slice.

Nutrition:

- Calories: 238
- Fa:t 7.7 g
- Protein: 7.2 g
- Carbohydrates: 35.5 g
- Fiber: 1.9 g

Chapter 11. Poultry and Meat

67. Chicken and Lemongrass Sauce

Preparation time: 15 minutes

Cooking time: 20 minutes

Servings: 3

Ingredients:

- 1 tbsp dried dill
- 1 tsp butter, melted
- 1/2 tsp lemongrass
- 1/2 tsp cayenne pepper
- 1 tsp tomato sauce
- 3 tbsp sour cream
- 1 tsp salt
- 10 oz chicken fillet, cubed

Directions:

1. Make the sauce: in the saucepan whisk together lemongrass, tomato sauce, sour cream, salt, pepper, and dried dill.
2. Bring the sauce to a boil.
3. Meanwhile, pour melted butter into the skillet.
4. Add cubed chicken fillet and roast it for 5 minutes. Stir it from time to time.
5. Then place the chicken cubes in the hot sauce.
6. Close the lid and cook the meal for 10 minutes over low heat.

Nutrition:

- Calories: 166
- Fat: 8.2 g
- Protein: 21 g
- Carbohydrates: 1.1 g
- Fiber: 0.2 g

68. Sesame Chicken With Black Rice, Broccoli, and Snap Peas

Preparation time: 10 minutes

Cooking time: 25 minutes

Servings: 3

Ingredients:

- 2/3 cup black rice
- 2 (200 g) chicken breast fillets
- 2 cups chopped broccoli
- 200 g snap peas, trimmed
- 1 1/2 cups packed watercress leaves
- 1 1/2 tbsp salt-reduced tamari
- 1 tbsp sesame seeds
- 2 tbsp tahini
- 1/2 tsp raw honey
- Olive oil to taste

Directions:

1. Boil rice in a saucepan for about 15 minutes or until al dente; drain.
2. Coat chicken fillets with sesame seeds and cook in hot oil in a skillet set over medium-high heat for about 5 minutes per side or until cooked through.
3. Let cool and slice. In the meantime, steam broccoli and peas until tender.
4. In a small bowl, whisk together tahini, tamari, and raw honey until very smooth. Divide

cooked black rice among serving bowls and top each with broccoli and peas. Top with chicken and watercress; drizzle each serving with tahini dressing. Enjoy!

Nutrition:

- Calories: 250
- Fat: 15.5 g
- Protein: 19.2 g
- Carbohydrates: 11.5 g
- Sugars: 3.7 g

69. Tasty Lamb Ribs

Preparation time: 10 minutes

Cooking time: 30 minutes

Servings: 4

Ingredients:

- 2 garlic cloves, minced
- 1/4 cup shallot, chopped
- 2 tbsp fish sauce
- 1/2 cup veggie stock
- 2 tbsp olive oil
- 1 and 1/2 tbsp lemon juice
- 1 tbsp coriander seeds, ground
- 1 tbsp ginger, grated
- Salt and black pepper to taste
- 2 lb lamb ribs

Directions:

1. In a roasting pan, combine the lamb with the garlic, shallots, and the rest of the ingredients, toss, introduce in the oven at 300°F and cook for 2 hours.
2. Divide the lamb between plates and serve with a side salad.

Nutrition:

- Calories: 293
- Fat: 9.1 g
- Protein: 24.2 g
- Carbohydrates: 16.7 g
- Fiber: 9.6 g

70. Saffron Beef

Preparation time: 5 minutes

Cooking time: 15 minutes

Servings: 3

Ingredients:

- 3/4 tsp saffron
- 3/4 tsp dried thyme
- 3/4 tsp ground coriander
- 1/4 tsp ground cinnamon
- 1 tbsp butter
- 1/3 tsp salt
- 9 oz beef sirloin

Directions:

1. Rub the beef sirloin with dried thyme, ground coriander, saffron, ground cinnamon, and salt.
2. Leave the meat for at least 10 minutes to soak all the spices.
3. Then preheat the grill to 395°F.
4. Place the beef sirloin on the grill and cook it for 5 minutes.
5. Then spread the meat with butter carefully and cook for 10 minutes more. Flip it on another side from time to time.

Nutrition:

- Calories: 291
- Fat: 13.8 g
- Protein: 38.8 g
- Carbohydrates: 0.6 g
- Fiber: 0.3 g

71. Chicken and Butter Sauce

Preparation time: 15 minutes

Cooking time: 30 minutes

Servings: 5

Ingredients:

- 1 lb chicken fillet

- 1/3 cup butter, softened
- 1 tbsp rosemary
- 1/2 tsp thyme
- 1 tsp salt
- 1/2 lemon

Directions:

1. Churn together thyme, salt, and rosemary.
2. Chop the chicken fillet roughly and mix it up with churned butter mixture.
3. Place the prepared chicken in the baking dish.
4. Squeeze the lemon over the chicken.
5. Chop the squeezed lemon and add to the baking dish.
6. Cover the chicken with foil and bake it for 20 minutes at 365°F.
7. Then discard the foil and bake the chicken for 10 minutes more.

Nutrition:

- Calories: 285
- Fat: 19.1 g
- Protein: 26.5 g
- Carbohydrates: 1 g
- Fiber: 0.5 g

72. Lemon and Garlic Barbecued Ocean Trout With Green Salad

Preparation time: 5 minutes

Cooking time: 10 minutes

Servings: 3

Ingredients:

- 1.5 kg piece trout fillet
- 2 tbsp lemon juice
- 4 garlic cloves, sliced
- 1 long red chili, sliced
- 2 tbsp chopped capers
- 1/2 cup fresh parsley
- 1/2 cup olive oil
- Lemon wedges to taste
- Salad greens for serving

Directions:

1. Brush the trout with 2 tbsp oil and then place it, skin-side up on a barbecue plate.
2. Cook over the preheated barbecue on high for about 5 minutes and then turn it over. Close the hood and cook on medium heat for another 15 minutes or until cooked through. Transfer to a plate.
3. In a pan, heat the remaining oil and then sauté garlic until lightly browned. Remove from heat and stir in chili, capers, and fresh lemon juice; drizzle over the fish and then sprinkle with parsley. Serve garnished with fresh lemon wedges.

Nutrition:

- Calories: 250
- Fat: 15.5 g
- Protein: 19.2 g
- Carbohydrates: 11.5 g
- Sugars: 3.7 g

73. Chicken and Black Beans

Preparation time: 10 minutes

Cooking time: 20 minutes

Servings: 3

Ingredients:

- 12 oz chicken breast, skinless, boneless, chopped
- 1 tbsp taco seasoning
- 1 tbsp nut oil
- 1/2 tsp cayenne pepper
- 1/2 tsp salt
- 1/2 tsp garlic, chopped
- 1/2 red onion, sliced
- 1/3 cup black beans, canned, rinsed
- 1/2 cup Mozzarella, shredded

Directions:

1. Rub the chopped chicken breast with taco seasoning, salt, and cayenne pepper.

2. Place the chicken in the skillet, add nut oil and roast it for 10 minutes over medium heat. Mix up the chicken pieces from time to time to avoid burning.
3. After this, transfer the chicken to the plate.
4. Add sliced onion and garlic to the skillet. Roast the vegetables for 5 minutes. Stir them constantly. Then add black beans and stir well. Cook the ingredients for 2 minutes more.
5. Add the chopped chicken and mix up well. Top the meal with Mozzarella cheese.
6. Close the lid and cook the meal for 3 minutes.

Nutrition:

- Calories: 209
- Fat: 6.4 g
- Protein: 22.7 g
- Carbohydrates: 13.7 g
- Fiber: 2.8 g

74. Sweet Chipotle Grilled Beef Ribs

Preparation time: 10 minutes

Cooking time: 35 minutes

Servings: 4

Ingredients:

- 4 tbsp sugar-free BBQ sauce + extra for serving
- 2 tbsp erythritol
- Pink salt and black pepper to taste
- 2 tbsp olive oil
- 2 tsp chipotle powder
- 1 tsp garlic powder
- 1 lb. beef spare ribs

Directions:

1. Mix the erythritol, salt, pepper, oil, chipotle, and garlic powder. Brush on the meaty sides of the ribs and wrap in foil. Sit for 30 minutes to marinate.
2. Preheat oven to 400°F. Place wrapped ribs on a baking sheet and cook for 40 minutes until cooked through. Remove ribs and aluminum foil, brush with BBQ sauce, and brown under the broiler for 10 minutes on both sides. Slice and serve with extra BBQ sauce and lettuce tomato salad.

Nutrition:

- Calories: 395
- Fat: 33 g
- Protein: 21 g
- Carbohydrates: 3 g

75. Grilled Sirloin Steak With Sauce Diane

Preparation time: 10 minutes

Cooking time: 25 minutes

Servings: 6

Ingredients:

Sirloin steak:

- 1 1/2 lb. sirloin steak
- Salt and black pepper to taste
- 1 tsp olive oil

Sauce Diane:

- 1 tbsp olive oil
- 1 garlic clove, minced
- 1 cup sliced porcini mushrooms
- 1 small onion, finely diced
- 2 tbsp butter
- 1 tbsp Dijon mustard
- 2 tbsp Worcestershire sauce
- 2 cups heavy cream

Directions:

1. Put a grill pan over high heat and as it heats, brush the steak with oil, sprinkle with salt and pepper, and rub the seasoning into the meat with your hands. Cook the steak in the pan for 4 minutes on each side for medium-rare and transfer to a chopping board to rest for 4 minutes before slicing. Reserve the juice.
2. Heat the oil in a frying pan over medium heat and sauté the onion for 3 minutes. Add the butter, garlic, and mushrooms, and cook for 2

minutes. Add the Worcestershire sauce, the reserved juice, and mustard.

3. Stir and cook for 1 minute. Swirl the pan and add the cream. Let it simmer to thicken for about 3 minutes. Adjust the taste with salt and pepper. Spoon the sauce over the steaks slices and serve with celeriac mash.

Nutrition:

- Calories: 434
- Fat: 17 g
- Protein: 36 g
- Carbohydrates: 2.9 g

76. Easy Zucchini Beef Lasagna

Preparation time: 25 minutes

Cooking time: 1 hour

Servings: 4

Ingredients:

- 1 lb. ground beef
- 2 large zucchinis, sliced lengthwise
- 3 garlic cloves
- 1 medium white onion, chopped
- 3 tomatoes, chopped
- Salt and black pepper to taste
- 2 tsp sweet paprika
- 1 tsp dried thyme
- 1 tsp dried basil
- 1 cup mozzarella cheese, shredded
- 1 tbsp olive oil

Directions:

1. Preheat the oven to 370°F. Heat the olive oil in a skillet over medium heat. Cook the beef for 4 minutes while breaking any lumps as you stir. Top with onion, garlic, tomatoes, salt, paprika, and pepper. Stir and continue cooking for 5 minutes. Lay 1/3 of the zucchini slices in the baking dish.
2. Top with 1/3 of the beef mixture and repeat the layering process two more times with the same quantities. Season with basil and thyme. Sprinkle the mozzarella cheese on top and tuck the baking dish in the oven. Bake for 35 minutes. Remove the lasagna and let it rest for 10 minutes before serving.

Nutrition:

- Calories: 344
- Fat: 17.8 g
- Protein: 40.4 g
- Carbohydrates: 2.9 g

77. Rib Roast With Roasted Shallots and Garlic

Preparation time: 15 minutes

Cooking time: 40 minutes

Servings: 6

Ingredients:

- 5 lb. beef rib roast, on the bone
- 3 heads of garlic, cut in half
- 3 tbsp olive oil
- 6 shallots, peeled and halved
- 2 lemons, zested and juiced
- 3 tbsp mustard seeds
- 3 tbsp swerve
- Salt and black pepper to taste
- 3 tbsp thyme leaves

Directions:

1. Preheat the oven to 400°F. Place garlic heads and shallots in a roasting dish, toss with olive oil, and bake for 15 minutes. Pour lemon juice on them. Score shallow crisscrosses patterns on the meat and set them aside.
2. Mix swerve, mustard seeds, thyme, salt, pepper, and lemon zest to make a rub and apply it all over the beef. Place the beef on the shallots and garlic and cook in the oven for 20 minutes. Once ready, remove the dish, and let sit covered for 15 minutes before slicing. Serve.

Nutrition:

- Calories: 222
- Fat: 29.7 g

- Protein: 5 g
- Carbohydrates: 3 g

78. Beef Meatballs

Preparation time: 23 minutes

Cooking time: 35 minutes

Servings: 4

Ingredients:

- 1/2 cup pork rinds, crushed
- 1 egg
- Salt and black pepper to taste
- 1 1/2 lb. ground beef
- 10 oz canned onion soup
- 1 tbsp almond flour
- 1/4 cup sugar-free ketchup
- 3 tsp Worcestershire sauce
- 1/2 tsp dry mustard
- 1/4 cup water

Directions:

1. In a bowl, combine 1/3 cup of the onion soup with the beef, pepper, pork rinds, egg, and salt. Shape the mixture into 12 meatballs. Heat a greased pan over medium heat. Brown the meatballs for 12 minutes.
2. In a separate bowl, combine the rest of the soup with the almond flour, dry mustard, ketchup, Worcestershire sauce, and 1/4 cup water. Pour this over the beef meatballs, cover the pan, and cook for 10 minutes as you stir occasionally. Split among bowls and serve.

Nutrition:

- Calories: 332
- Fat: 18 g
- Protein: 25 g
- Carbohydrates: 7 g

79. Pot Roast

Preparation time: 30 minutes

Cooking time: 2 hours 20 minutes

Servings: 6

Ingredients:

- 1 1/2 lb. brisket
- 2 tbsp olive oil
- 8 baby carrots, peeled
- 2 medium red onions, quartered
- 1 celery stalk, cut into chunks
- Salt and black pepper to taste
- 2 bay leaves

Directions:

1. Preheat oven to 370ºF. Heat the olive oil in a large skillet over medium heat. Season the brisket with salt and pepper.
2. Brown the meat on both sides for 8 minutes. After, transfer to a deep casserole dish. In the dish, arrange the carrots, onions, celery, and bay leaves around the brisket.
3. Cover the pot and cook in the oven for 2 hours. When ready, remove the casserole. Transfer the beef to a chopping board and cut it into thick slices. Serve the beef and vegetables with a drizzle of the sauce.

Nutrition:

- Calories: 302.2
- Fat: 22.7 g
- Protein: 8 g
- Carbohydrates: 9.3 g

80. Beef Tripe Pot

Preparation time: 10 minutes

Cooking time: 1 hour 30 minutes

Servings: 6

Ingredients:

- 1 1/2 lb. beef tripe, cleaned
- 4 cups buttermilk
- Salt and black pepper to taste
- 3 tbsp olive oil
- 2 onions, sliced
- 4 garlic cloves, minced

- 3 tomatoes, diced
- 1 tsp paprika
- 2 chili peppers, minced

Directions:

1. Put the tripe in a bowl and cover it with buttermilk. Refrigerate for 3 hours to extract bitterness and a gamey taste.
2. Remove from buttermilk, drain and rinse well under cold running water. Place in a pot over medium heat and cover with water. Bring to a boil and cook about for 1 hour until tender. Remove the tripe with a perforated spoon and let cool. Strain the broth and reserve. Chop the cooled tripe.
3. Heat the oil in a skillet over medium heat. Sauté the onions, garlic, and chili peppers for 3 minutes until soft. Stir in the paprika and add in the tripe. Cook for 5 to 6 minutes. Include the tomatoes and 4 cups of the reserved tripe broth and cook for 10 minutes. Adjust the seasoning with salt and pepper. Serve.

Nutrition:

- Calories: 248
- Fat: 12.8 g
- Protein: 8 g
- Carbohydrates: 4 g

81. Beef Stovies

Preparation time: 12 minutes

Cooking time: 45 minutes

Servings: 4

Ingredients:

- 1 lb. ground beef
- 1 large onion, chopped
- 2 parsnips, peeled and chopped
- 1 large carrot, chopped
- 2 tbsp olive oil
- 2 garlic cloves, minced
- Salt and black pepper to taste
- 1 cup chicken broth
- 1/4 tsp allspice
- 2 tsp fresh rosemary, chopped
- 1 tbsp Worcestershire sauce
- 1/2 small cabbage, shredded

Directions:

1. Heat the olive oil in a skillet over medium heat and cook the beef for 4 minutes. Season with salt and pepper, stirring occasionally while breaking the lumps in it.
2. Add onion, garlic, carrot, rosemary, and parsnips.
3. Stir and cook for a minute, and pour in the chicken broth, allspice, and Worcestershire sauce.
4. Reduce the heat to low and cook for 20 minutes. Stir in the cabbage, season with salt and black pepper, and cook further for 15 minutes. Turn the heat off, plate the stovies, and serve warm.

Nutrition:

- Calories: 316
- Fat: 18 g
- Protein: 14 g
- Carbohydrates: 3 g

82. Festive Turkey Rouladen

Preparation time: 15 minutes

Cooking time: 30 minutes

Servings: 5

Ingredients:

- 2 lb. turkey fillet, marinated and cut into 10 pieces
- 10 strips prosciutto
- 1/2 tsp chili powder
- 1 tsp marjoram
- 1 sprig of rosemary, finely chopped
- 1 tsp garlic, finely minced
- 1 1/2 tbsp butter, room temperature
- 1 tbsp Dijon mustard
- Sea salt and freshly ground black pepper, to your liking

Directions:

1. Start by preheating your oven to 430°F.
2. Pat the turkey dry and cook in hot butter for about 3 minutes per side. Add in the mustard, chili powder, marjoram, rosemary, wine, and garlic.
3. Continue to cook for 2 minutes more. Wrap each turkey piece into one prosciutto strip and secure with toothpicks. Add salt and pepper to taste.
4. Roast in the preheated oven for about 30 minutes.

Nutrition:

- Calories: 286
- Fat: 9.7 g
- Protein: 39.9 g
- Carbohydrates: 6.9 g
- Fiber: 0.3 g

83. Pan-Fried Chorizo Sausage

Preparation time: 10 minutes

Cooking time: 20 minutes

Servings: 4

Ingredients:

- 16 oz smoked turkey chorizo
- 1 1/2 cups Asiago cheese, grated
- 1 tsp oregano
- 1 tsp basil
- 1 cup tomato puree
- 4 scallion stalks, chopped
- 1 tsp garlic paste
- Sea salt and ground black pepper to taste
- 1 tbsp dry sherry
- 1 tbsp extra-virgin olive oil
- 2 tbsp fresh coriander, roughly chopped

Directions:

1. Heat the oil in a frying pan over moderately high heat. Now, brown the turkey chorizo, crumbling with a fork for about 5 minutes.
2. Add in the other ingredients, except for cheese; continue to cook for 10 minutes more or until cooked through. Add cheese.

Nutrition:

- Calories: 330
- Fat: 17.2 g
- Protein: 34.4 g
- Carbohydrates: 4.5 g
- Fiber: 1.6 g

84. Chinese Bok Choy and Turkey Soup

Preparation time: 15 minutes

Cooking time: 40 minutes

Servings: 8

Ingredients:

- 1/2 lb. baby Bok choy, sliced into quarters lengthwise
- 2 lb. turkey carcass
- 1 tbsp olive oil
- 1/2 cup leeks, chopped
- 1 celery rib, chopped
- 2 carrots, sliced
- 6 cups turkey stock
- Himalayan salt and black pepper, to taste

Directions:

1. In a heavy-bottomed pot, heat the olive oil until sizzling. Once hot, sauté the celery, carrots, leek, and Bok Choy for about 6 minutes.
2. Add the salt, pepper, turkey, and stock; bring to a boil.
3. Turn the heat to simmer. Continue to cook, partially covered, for about 35 minutes.

Nutrition:

- Calories: 211
- Fat: 11.8 g
- Protein: 23.7 g
- Carbohydrates: 3.1 g
- Fiber: 0.9 g

85. Herby Chicken Meatloaf

Preparation time: 20 minutes

Cooking time: 30 minutes

Servings: 6

Ingredients:

- 2 1/2 lb. ground chicken
- 3 tbsp flaxseed meal
- 2 large eggs
- 2 tbsp olive oil
- 1 lemon, 1 tbsp juiced
- 1/4 cup chopped parsley
- 1/4 cup chopped oregano
- 4 garlic cloves, minced
- Lemon slices to garnish

Directions:

1. Preheat oven to 400°F. In a bowl, combine ground chicken and flaxseed meal; set aside. In a small bowl, whisk the eggs with olive oil, lemon juice, parsley, oregano, and garlic.
2. Pour the mixture onto the chicken mixture and mix well. Spoon into a greased loaf pan and press to fit. Bake for 40 minutes.
3. Remove the pan, drain the liquid, and let cool a bit. Slice, garnish with lemon slices, and serve.

Nutrition:

- Calories: 362
- Fat: 24 g
- Protein: 35 g
- Carbohydrates: 1.3 g

86. Lovely Pulled Chicken Egg Bites

Preparation time: 15 minutes

Cooking time: 30 minutes

Servings: 4

Ingredients:

- 2 tbsp butter
- 1 chicken breast
- 2 tbsp chopped green onions
- 1/2 tsp red chili flakes
- 12 eggs
- 1/4 cup grated Monterey Jack

Directions:

1. Preheat the oven to 400°F. Line a 12-hole muffin tin with cupcake liners. Melt butter in a skillet over medium heat and cook the chicken until brown on each side, 10 minutes.
2. Transfer to a plate and shred with 2 forks. Divide between muffin holes along with green onions and red chili flakes.
3. Crack an egg into each muffin hole and scatter the cheese on top. Bake for 15 minutes until the eggs are set. Serve.

Nutrition:

- Calories: 393
- Fat: 27 g
- Protein: 34 g
- Carbohydrates: 0.5 g

Chapter 12. Fish and Seafood

87. Shrimp With Garlic

Preparation time: 10 minutes

Cooking time: 25 minutes

Servings: 2

Ingredients:

- 1 lb. shrimp
- 1/4 tsp baking soda
- 2 tbsp oil
- 2 tsp minced garlic
- 1/4 cup vermouth
- 2 tbsp unsalted butter
- 1 tsp parsley
- Salt to taste

- 1 tbsp Red pepper flakes

Directions:

1. In a bowl toss shrimp with baking soda and salt, and let it stand for a couple of minutes.
2. In a skillet heat olive oil and add shrimp.
3. Add garlic, and red pepper flakes and cook for 1 to 2 minutes.
4. Add vermouth, and butter, and cook for another 4 to 5 minutes.
5. When ready remove from heat and serve. Add parsley.

Nutrition:

- Calories: 289
- Fat: 17 g
- Protein: 7 g
- Carbohydrates: 2 g
- Fiber: 2 g
- Sodium: 163 mg
- Cholesterol: 3 mg

88. Sabich Sandwich

Preparation time: 5 minutes

Cooking time: 15 minutes

Servings: 2

Ingredients:

- 2 tomatoes
- Olive oil to taste
- 1/2 lb. eggplant
- 1/4 cucumber
- 1 tbsp lemon
- 1 tbsp parsley
- 1/4 head cabbage
- 2 tbsp wine vinegar
- 2 pitas bread
- 1/2 cup hummus
- 1/4 tahini sauce
- 2 hard-boiled eggs

Directions:

1. In a skillet fry eggplant slices until tender.
2. In a bowl add tomatoes, cucumber, parsley, and lemon juice, and season the salad.
3. In another bowl toss cabbage with vinegar.
4. In each pita pocket add hummus, eggplant, and drizzle tahini sauce.
5. Top with eggs.

Nutrition:

- Calories: 269
- Fat: 14 g
- Protein: 7 g
- Carbohydrates: 2 g
- Fiber: 2 g
- Sodium: 183 mg
- Cholesterol: 3 mg

89. Salmon With Vegetables

Preparation time: 10 minutes

Cooking time: 15 minutes

Servings: 4

Ingredients:

- 2 tbsp olive oil
- 2 carrots
- 1 head fennel
- 2 squashes
- 1/4 onion
- 1-inch ginger
- 2 cups water
- 2 parsley sprigs
- 2 tarragon sprigs
- 6 oz. salmon fillets
- 1 cup cherry tomatoes
- 1 scallion

Directions:

1. In a skillet heat olive oil, add fennel, squash, onion, ginger, and carrot, and cook until vegetables are soft.
2. Add wine, water, parsley, and tarragon, and cook for another 4 to 5 minutes.
3. Season salmon fillets and place in the pan.
4. Cook for 5 minutes per side or until is ready.

5. Transfer salmon to a bowl, spoon tomatoes and scallion around salmon and serve.

Nutrition:

- Calories: 301
- Fat: 17 g
- Protein: 8 g
- Carbohydrates: 2 g
- Fiber: 4 g
- Sodium: 201 mg
- Cholesterol: 13 mg

90. Crispy Fish

Preparation time: 5 minutes

Cooking time: 15 minutes

Servings: 4

Ingredients:

- 4 Thick fish fillets
- 1/4 cup all-purpose flour
- 1 egg
- 1 cup bread crumbs
- 2 tbsp vegetables
- Lemon wedge to taste

Directions:

1. In a dish add flour, egg, and breadcrumbs in different dishes and set aside.
2. Dip each fish fillet into the flour, egg, and then bread crumbs bowl.
3. Place each fish fillet in a heated skillet and cook for 4 to 5 minutes per side.
4. When ready remove from pan and serve with lemon wedges and vegetables.

Nutrition:

- Calories: 189
- Fat: 17 g
- Protein: 7 g
- Carbohydrates: 2 g
- Fiber: 0 g
- Sodium: 163 mg
- Cholesterol: 73 mg

91. Moules Marinieres

Preparation time: 10 minutes

Cooking time: 30 minutes

Servings: 4

Ingredients:

- 2 tbsp unsalted butter
- 1 leek
- 1 shallot
- 2 garlic cloves
- 2 bay leaves
- 2 lb. mussels
- 2 tbsp mayonnaise
- 1 tbsp lemon zest
- 2 tbsp parsley
- 1 sourdough bread

Directions:

1. In a saucepan melt butter, add leeks, garlic, bay leaves, shallot, and white wine, and cook until vegetables are soft.
2. Bring to a boil, add mussels, and cook for 1 to 2 minutes.
3. Transfer mussels to a bowl and cover.
4. Whisk in the remaining butter with mayonnaise and return mussels to the pot.
5. Add bread, parsley, lemon zest, and stir to combine.

Nutrition:

- Calories: 321
- Fat: 17 g
- Protein: 9 g
- Carbohydrates: 2 g
- Fiber: 2 g
- Sodium: 312 mg
- Cholesterol: 13 mg

92. Steamed Mussels With Coconut-Curry

Preparation time: 15 minutes

Cooking time: 20 minutes

Servings: 4

Ingredients:

- 6 sprigs of cilantro
- 2 garlic cloves
- 2 shallots
- 1/4 tsp coriander seeds
- 1/4 tsp red chili flakes
- 1 tsp zest and lime juice
- 1 can coconut milk
- 1 tbsp vegetable oil
- 1 tbsp curry paste
- 1 tbsp brown sugar
- 1 tbsp fish sauce
- 2 lb. mussels
- Salt to taste
- Cilantro leaves to taste

Directions:

1. In a bowl combine lime zest, cilantro stems, shallot, garlic, coriander seed, chili, and salt.
2. In a saucepan heat oil and add, garlic, shallots, pounded paste, and curry paste.
3. Cook for 3 to 4 minutes, add coconut milk, sugar, and fish sauce.
4. Bring to a simmer and add mussels.
5. Stir in lime juice, and cilantro leaves and cook for a couple of more minutes.
6. When ready remove from heat and serve.

Nutrition:

- Calories: 209
- Fat: 7 g
- Protein: 17 g
- Carbohydrates: 6 g
- Fiber: 2 g
- Sodium: 193 mg
- Cholesterol: 13 mg

93. Tuna Noodle Casserole

Preparation time: 15 minutes

Cooking time: 20 minutes

Servings: 4

Ingredients:

- 2 oz egg noodles
- 4 oz Fraiche
- 1 egg
- 1 tsp cornstarch
- 1 tbsp juice from 1 lemon
- 1 can of tuna
- 1 cup peas
- 1/4 cup parsley

Directions:

1. Place noodles in a saucepan with water and bring to a boil.
2. In a bowl combine egg, crème Fraiche, cornstarch, and lemon juice, and whisk well.
3. When the noodles are cooked add the crème Fraiche mixture to the skillet and mix well.
4. Add tuna, peas, parsley lemon juice, and mix well.
5. When ready remove from heat and serve.

Nutrition:

- Calories: 214
- Fat: 7 g
- Protein: 19 g
- Carbohydrates: 2 g
- Fiber: 2 g
- Sodium: 308 g
- Cholesterol: 73 mg

94. Salmon Burgers

Preparation time: 10 minutes

Cooking time: 15 minutes

Servings: 4

Ingredients:

- 1 lb. salmon fillets
- 1 onion
- 1/4 dill fronds
- 1 tbsp honey
- 1 tbsp horseradish
- 1 tbsp mustard
- 1 tbsp mayonnaise
- 1 tbsp olive oil
- 2 toasted split rolls
- 1 avocado
- Salt and pepper to taste

Directions:

1. Place salmon fillets in a blender and blend until smooth, transfer to a bowl, add onion, dill, honey, and horseradish, and mix well.
2. Add salt, pepper, and form 4 patties.
3. In a bowl combine mustard, honey, mayonnaise, and dill.
4. In a skillet heat oil add salmon patties and cook for 2 to 3 minutes per side.
5. When ready remove from heat.
6. Divided lettuce and onion between the buns.
7. Place salmon patty on top and spoon mustard mixture and avocado slices
8. Serve when ready.

Nutrition:

- Calories: 189
- Fat: 7 g
- Protein: 12 g
- Carbohydrates: 6 g
- Fiber: 4 g
- Sodium: 293 mg
- Cholesterol: 3 mg

95. Seared Scallops

Preparation time: 15 minutes

Cooking time: 20 minutes

Servings: 4

Ingredients:

- 1 lb. sea scallops
- 1 tbsp canola oil

Directions:

1. Season scallops and refrigerate for a couple of minutes.
2. In a skillet heat oil, add scallops, and cook for 1 to 2 minutes per side.

3. When ready remove from heat and serve.

Nutrition:

- Calories: 283
- Fat: 8 g
- Protein: 9 g
- Carbohydrates: 10 g
- Fiber: 2 g
- Sodium: 271 mg
- Cholesterol: 3 mg

96. Black COD

Preparation time: 15 minutes

Cooking time: 20 minutes

Servings: 4

Ingredients:

- 1/4 cup miso paste
- 1/4 cup sake
- 1 tbsp mirin
- 1 tsp soy sauce
- 1 tbsp olive oil
- 4 black cod filets

Directions:

1. In a bowl combine miso, mirin, soy sauce, oil, and sake.
2. Rub mixture over cod fillets and let it marinade for 20 to 30 minutes.
3. Adjust broiler and broil cod filets for 10 to 12 minutes.
4. When fish is cook remove and serve.

Nutrition:

- Calories: 231
- Fat: 15 g
- Protein: 8 g
- Carbohydrates: 2 g
- Fiber: 2 g
- Sodium: 298 mg
- Cholesterol: 13 mg

97. Miso-Glazed Salmon

Preparation time: 10 minutes

Cooking time: 40 minutes

Servings: 4

Ingredients:

- 1/4 cup red miso
- 1/4 cup sake
- 1 tbsp soy sauce
- 1 tbsp vegetable oil
- 4 salmon fillets

Directions:

1. In a bowl combine sake, oil, soy sauce, and miso.
2. Rub mixture over salmon fillets and marinade for 20 to 30 minutes.
3. Preheat a broiler.
4. Broil salmon for 5 to 10 minutes.
5. When ready remove and serve.

Nutrition:

- Calories: 198
- Fat: 10 g
- Protein: 6 g
- Carbohydrates: 5 g
- Fiber: 2 g
- Sodium: 257 mg
- Cholesterol: 12 mg

98. Arugula and Sweet Potato Salad

Preparation time: 10 minutes

Cooking time: 20 minutes

Servings: 4

Ingredients:

- 1 lb. sweet potatoes
- 1 cup walnuts
- 1 tbsp olive oil
- 1 cup water

- 1 tbsp soy sauce
- 3 cups arugula

Directions:

1. Bake potatoes at 400°F until tender, remove and set aside.
2. In a bowl drizzle, walnuts with olive oil and microwave for 2 to 3 minutes or until toasted.
3. In a bowl combine all salad ingredients and mix well.
4. Pour over the soy sauce and serve.

Nutrition:

- Calories: 189
- Fat: 7 g
- Protein: 10 g
- Carbohydrates: 2 g
- Fiber: 2 g
- Sodium: 301 mg
- Cholesterol: 13 mg

99. Nicoise Salad

Preparation time: 15 minutes

Cooking time: 10 minutes

Servings: 4

Ingredients:

- 1 oz red potatoes
- 1 package of green beans
- 2 eggs
- 1/2 cup tomatoes
- 2 tbsp wine vinegar
- 1/4 tsp salt
- 1/2 tsp pepper
- 1/2 tsp thyme
- 1/4 cup olive oil
- 6 oz tuna
- 1/4 cup Kalamata olives

Directions:

1. In a bowl combine all ingredients together.
2. Add salad dressing and serve.

Nutrition:

- Calories: 189
- Fat: 7 g
- Protein: 15 g
- Carbohydrates: 2 g
- Fiber: 2 g
- Sodium: 321 mg
- Cholesterol: 13 mg

100. Shrimp Curry

Preparation time: 15 minutes

Cooking time: 20 minutes

Servings: 4

Ingredients:

- 2 tbsp peanut oil
- 1/4 onion
- 2 garlic cloves
- 1 tsp ginger
- 1 tsp cumin
- 1 tsp turmeric
- 1 tsp paprika
- 1/4 red chili powder
- 1 can of tomatoes
- 1 can coconut milk
- 1 lb. peeled shrimp
- 1 tbsp cilantro

Directions:

1. In a skillet add onion and cook for 4 to 5 minutes.
2. Add ginger, cumin, garlic, turmeric, chili, and paprika and cook on low heat.
3. Pour the tomatoes, and coconut milk and simmer for 10 to 12 minutes.
4. Stir in shrimp, and cilantro, and cook for 2 to 3 minutes.
5. When ready remove and serve.

Nutrition:

- Calories: 178
- Fat: 17 g
- Protein: 9 g

- Carbohydrates: 3 g
- Sodium: 297 mg
- Cholesterol: 3 mg

101. Salmon Pasta

Preparation time: 10 minutes

Cooking time: 25 minutes

Servings: 2

Ingredients:

- 5 tbsp butter
- 1/4 onion
- 1 tbsp all-purpose flour
- 1 tsp garlic powder
- 2 cups skim milk
- 1/4 cup Romano cheese
- 1 cup green peas
- 1/4 cup canned mushrooms
- 8 oz salmon
- 1 package of penne pasta

Directions:

1. Bring a pot with water to a boil.
2. Add pasta and cook for 10 to 12 minutes.
3. In a skillet melt butter, add onion, and sauté until tender.
4. Stir in garlic powder, flour, milk, and cheese.
5. Add mushrooms, and peas and cook on low heat for 4 to 5 minutes.
6. Toss in salmon and cook for another 2 to 3 minutes.
7. When ready serve with cooked pasta.

Nutrition:

- Calories: 211
- Fat: 18 g
- Protein: 17 g
- Carbohydrates: 7 g
- Fiber: 3 g
- Sodium: 289 mg
- Cholesterol: 13 mg

102. Crab Legs

Preparation time: 5 minutes

Cooking time: 20 minutes

Servings: 3

Ingredients:

- 3 lb. crab legs
- 1/4 cup salted butter, melted and divided
- 1/2 lemon, juiced
- 1/4 tsp garlic powder

Directions:

1. In a bowl, toss the crab legs and 2 tbsp melted butter together. Place the crab legs in the basket of the fryer.
2. Cook at 400°F for 15 minutes, giving the basket a good shake halfway through.
3. Combine the remaining butter with lemon juice and garlic powder.
4. Crack open the cooked crab legs and remove the meat. Serve with the butter dip on the side and enjoy!

Nutrition:

- Calories: 392
- Fat: 10 g
- Protein: 18 g
- Sugar: 8 g

103. Crusty Pesto Salmon

Preparation time: 5 minutes

Cooking time: 15 minutes

Servings: 2

Ingredients:

- 1/4 cup breadcrumbs, roughly chopped
- 1/4 cup pesto
- 2 x 4 oz salmon fillets
- 2 tbsp unsalted butter, melted

Directions:

1. Mix the breadcrumbs and pesto together.
2. Place the salmon fillets in a round baking dish, roughly 6 inches in diameter.
3. Brush the fillets with butter, followed by the pesto mixture, ensuring to coat both the top and bottom. Put the baking dish inside the fryer.
4. Cook for twelve minutes at 390°F.
5. The salmon is ready when it flakes easily when prodded with a fork. Serve warm.

Nutrition:

- Calories: 290
- Fat: 11 g
- Protein: 20 g
- Sugar: 9 g

104. Buttery Cod

Preparation time: 10 minutes

Cooking time: 12 minutes

Servings: 2

Ingredients:

- 2 x 4 oz cod fillets
- 2 tbsp salted butter, melted
- 1 tsp Old Bay seasoning
- 1/2 medium lemon, sliced

Directions:

1. Place the cod fillets in a skillet.
2. Brush with melted butter, season with Old Bay, and top with a few lemon wedges.
3. Wrap the fish in aluminum foil and place it in your deep fryer.
4. Cook for 8 minutes at 350°F.
5. The cod is done when it is easily peeled. Serve hot.

Nutrition:

- Calories: 394
- Fat: 5 g
- Protein: 12 g
- Sugar: 4 g

105. Sesame Tuna Steak

Preparation time: 5 minutes

Cooking time: 12 minutes

Servings: 2

Ingredients:

- 1 tbsp coconut oil, melted
- 2 x 6 oz tuna steaks
- 1/2 tsp garlic powder
- 2 tsp black sesame seeds
- 2 tsp white sesame seeds

Directions:

1. Apply the coconut oil to the tuna steaks with a brunch, then season with garlic powder.
2. Combine the black and white sesame seeds. Embed them in the tuna steaks, covering the fish all over. Place the tuna into your air fryer.
3. Cook for 8 minutes at 400°F, turning the fish halfway through.
4. The tuna steaks are ready when they have reached a temperature of 145°F. Serve straight away.

Nutrition:

- Calories: 160
- Fat: 6 g
- Protein: 26 g
- Sugar: 7 g

106. Lemon Garlic Shrimp

Preparation time: 10 minutes

Cooking time: 15 minutes

Servings: 2

Ingredients:

- 1 medium lemon

- 1/2 lb. medium shrimp, shelled and deveined
- 1/2 tsp Old Bay seasoning
- 2 tbsp unsalted butter, melted
- 1/2 tsp minced garlic

Directions:

1. Grate the rind of the lemon into a bowl. Cut the lemon in half and juice it over the same bowl. Toss in the shrimp, Old Bay, garlic, and butter, mixing everything to make sure the shrimp is completely covered.
2. Transfer to a round baking dish roughly 6 inches wide, then place this dish in your fryer.
3. Cook at 400°F for 6 minutes. The shrimp is cooked when it turns a bright pink color.
4. Serve hot, drizzling any leftover sauce over the shrimp.

Nutrition:

- Calories: 490
- Fat: 9 g
- Protein: 12 g
- Sugar: 11 g

107. Foil Packet Salmon

Preparation time: 5 minutes

Cooking time: 15 minutes

Servings: 2

Ingredients:

- 2 x 4 oz skinless salmon fillets
- 2 tbsp unsalted butter, melted
- 1/2 tsp garlic powder
- 1 medium lemon
- 1/2 tsp dried dill

Directions:

1. Take a sheet of aluminum foil and cut it into two squares measuring roughly 5" x 5". Lay each of the salmon fillets at the center of each piece. Brush both fillets with 1 tbsp butter and season with 1/2 tsp garlic powder.
2. Halve the lemon and grate the skin of one-half over the fish. Cut four half-slices of lemon, using two to top each fillet. Season each fillet with 1/2 tsp dill.
3. Fold the tops and sides of the aluminum foil over the fish to create a kind of packet. Place each one in the fryer.
4. Cook for 20 minutes at 400°F.
5. The salmon is ready when it flakes easily. Serve hot.

Nutrition:

- Calories: 240
- Fat: 13 g
- Protein: 21 g

Chapter 13. Vegetables

108. Parsley Zucchini and Radishes

Preparation time: 5 minutes

Cooking time: 15 minutes

Servings: 4

Ingredients:

- 1 lb. zucchinis, cubed
- 1 cup radishes, halved
- 1 tbsp olive oil
- 1 tbsp balsamic vinegar
- 2 tomatoes, cubed
- 3 tbsp parsley, chopped
- Salt and black pepper to taste

Directions:

1. In a pan that fits your air fryer, mix the zucchinis with the radishes, oil, and the other ingredients, toss, introduce into the fryer and cook at 350°F for 15 minutes.
2. Divide between plates and serve as a side dish.

Nutrition:

- Calories: 170
- Fat: 6 g
- Protein: 6 g
- Carbohydrates: 5 g
- Fiber: 2 g

109. Cherry Tomatoes Sauté

Preparation time: 5 minutes

Cooking time: 15 minutes

Servings: 4

Ingredients:

- 1 tbsp olive oil
- 1 lb. cherry tomatoes, halved
- Juice of 1 lime
- 2 tbsp parsley, chopped
- A pinch of salt and black pepper

Directions:

1. In a pan that fits the air fryer, mix the tomatoes with the oil and the other ingredients, toss, introduce the pan to the machine and cook at 360°F for 15 minutes.
2. Divide between plates and serve.

Nutrition:

- Calories: 141
- Fat: 6 g
- Protein: 7 g
- Carbohydrates: 4 g
- Fiber: 2 g

110. Creamy Eggplant

Preparation time: 5 minutes

Cooking time: 20 minutes

Servings: 4

Ingredients:

- 2 lb. eggplants, roughly cubed
- 1 cup heavy cream
- 2 tbsp butter, melted
- Salt and black pepper to taste
- 1/2 tsp chili powder
- 1/2 tsp turmeric powder

Directions:

1. In a pan that fits the air fryer, mix the eggplants with the cream, butter, and the other ingredients, toss, introduce in the machine and cook at 370°F for 20 minutes.
2. Divide between plates and serve as a side dish.

Nutrition:

- Calories: 151
- Fat: 3 g
- Protein: 6 g
- Carbohydrates: 4 g
- Fiber: 2 g

111. Eggplant and Carrots Mix

Preparation time: 5 minutes

Cooking time: 25 minutes

Servings: 4

Ingredients:

- 1 lb. eggplants, roughly cubed
- 1 lb. baby carrots
- 1 cup heavy cream
- 1/2 tsp chili powder
- 1 tsp garlic powder
- 1 tbsp chives, chopped
- A pinch of salt and black pepper

Directions:

1. In a pan that fits your air fryer, mix the eggplants with the carrots, cream, and the other ingredients, toss, introduce to the air fryer and cook at 370°F for 25 minutes.
2. Divide between plates and serve as a side dish.

Nutrition:

- Calories: 129
- Fat: 6 g
- Protein: 8 g
- Carbohydrates: 5 g
- Fiber: 2 g

112. Parmesan Eggplants

Preparation time: 5 minutes

Cooking time: 20 minutes

Servings: 4

Ingredients:

- 1 lb. eggplants, roughly cubed
- 1 tbsp olive oil
- 1 tsp garlic powder
- 1 cup parmesan, grated
- A pinch of salt and black pepper
- Cooking spray

Directions:

1. In the air fryer's pan, mix the eggplants with the oil and the other ingredients except for the parmesan and toss.
2. Sprinkle the parmesan on top, put the pan in the machine, and cook at 370°F for 20 minutes.
3. Divide between plates and serve as a side dish.

Nutrition:

- Calories: 183
- Fat: 6 g
- Protein: 8 g
- Carbohydrates: 3 g
- Fiber: 2 g

113. Kale Sauté

Preparation time: 5 minutes

Cooking time: 15 minutes

Servings: 4

Ingredients:

- 1 tbsp avocado oil
- 1 lb. baby kale
- 1/2 cup heavy cream
- Salt and black pepper to taste
- 1/4 tsp chili powder
- 1 tbsp dill, chopped
- 1/4 cup walnuts, chopped

Directions:

1. In a pan that fits the air fryer, mix the kale with the oil, cream, and the other ingredients, toss, introduce the pan to the machine and cook at 360°F for 15 minutes.
2. Divide between plates and serve as a side dish.

Nutrition:

- Calories: 160
- Fat: 7 g
- Protein: 5 g
- Carbohydrates: 4 g
- Fiber: 2 g

114. Carrots Sauté

Preparation time: 5 minutes

Cooking time: 20 minutes

Servings: 4

Ingredients:

- 2 lb. baby carrots, peeled
- 1 tbsp balsamic vinegar
- 2 tbsp olive oil
- Salt and black pepper to taste
- 1 tbsp lemon juice
- 1/3 cup almonds, chopped
- 1/2 cup walnuts, chopped

Directions:

1. In a pan that fits the air fryer, mix the carrots with the vinegar, oil, and the other ingredients, toss, introduce the pan to the machine and cook at 380°F for 20 minutes.
2. Divide between plates and serve as a side dish.

Nutrition:

- Calories: 121
- Fat: 9 g
- Protein: 5 g
- Carbohydrates: 4 g
- Fiber: 2 g

115. Bok Choy and Sprouts

Preparation time: 5 minutes

Cooking time: 20 minutes

Servings: 4

Ingredients:

- 1 tbsp avocado oil
- 1 lb. Brussels sprouts, trimmed and halved
- 2 Bok Choy heads, trimmed and cut into strips
- 1 tbsp balsamic vinegar
- A pinch of salt and black pepper
- 1 tbsp dill, chopped

Directions:

1. In a pan that fits your air fryer, mix the sprouts with the Bok Choy and the other ingredients, toss, introduce the pan to the air fryer and cook at 380°F for 20 minutes.
2. Divide between plates and serve as a side dish.

Nutrition:

- Calories: 141
- Fat: 3 g
- Protein: 3 g
- Carbohydrates: 4 g
- Fiber: 2 g

116. Balsamic Radishes

Preparation time: 10 minutes

Cooking time: 20 minutes

Servings: 4

Ingredients:

- 1 lb. radishes, halved
- 1 tbsp balsamic vinegar
- 1 tsp chili powder
- 1 tbsp avocado oil
- Salt and black pepper to taste

Directions:

1. In a pan that fits the air fryer, combine the radishes with the vinegar and the other ingredients, toss, introduce the pan to the air fryer and cook at 380°F for 20 minutes.
2. Divide between plates and serve as a side dish.

Nutrition:

- Calories: 151
- Fat: 2 g
- Protein: 5 g
- Carbohydrates: 5 g
- Fiber: 3 g

117. Spaghetti Squash Casserole

Preparation time: 10 minutes

Cooking time: 20 minutes

Servings: 4

Ingredients:

- 12 oz spaghetti squash
- 1 tsp ground cinnamon
- 1/2 tsp salt
- 1 sweet potato, grated
- 1 tbsp almond flour
- 2 eggs
- 1 tbsp olive oil
- 1 onion, diced
- 1/4 tsp thyme

Directions:

1. Peel the spaghetti squash and chop it into 1/2-inch chunks.
2. Then place the squash in the air fryer basket.
3. Add salt and ground cinnamon.
4. Cook the sweet potatoes for 5 minutes at 380°F.
5. After this, make the layer of the grated potato over the sweet potato.
6. Beat the eggs in the bowl and whisk them.
7. Add almond flour and stir the mixture.
8. Then add olive oil, diced onion, and thyme.
9. Stir the mixture.
10. Pour it over the grated potato.
11. Cook the casserole for 15 minutes at 365°F.
12. When the time is over and the casserole is cooked—let it chill a little and serve!

Nutrition:

- Calories: 166
- Fat: 9.8 g
- Protein: 5.7 g
- Carbohydrates: 16.5 g
- Fiber: 2.6 g

118. Cinnamon Baby Carrot

Preparation time: 8 minutes

Cooking time: 15 minutes

Servings: 4

Ingredients:

- 1 lb. baby carrot
- 1 tbsp ground cinnamon
- 1 tsp ground ginger
- 1/4 cup almond milk
- 1 tbsp olive oil

Directions:

1. Wash the baby carrot carefully and sprinkle it with the ground cinnamon, ground ginger, and olive oil.
2. Stir the vegetables and transfer them to the air fryer basket.
3. Cook the baby carrot for 10 minutes at 380°F.
4. Then stir the baby carrots and add almond milk.
5. Stir the vegetables again and cook for 5 minutes more at the same temperature.
6. Let the cooked carrot chill a little and serve it!

Nutrition:

- Calories: 110
- Fat: 7.3 g
- Protein: 1.2 g
- Carbohydrates: 11.9 g
- Fiber: 4.6 g

119. Eggplant Tongues

Preparation time: 10 minutes

Cooking time: 14 minutes

Servings: 2

Ingredients:

- 2 eggplants
- 1 tsp minced garlic
- 1 tsp olive oil
- 1/4 tsp ground black pepper

Directions:

1. Wash the eggplants carefully and slice them.
2. Rub every eggplant slice with the minced garlic, olive oil, and ground black pepper.
3. Place the eggplants in the air fryer basket and cook for 7 minutes from each side at 375°F.
4. When the eggplant tongues are cooked—serve them immediately!

Nutrition:

- Calories: 160
- Fat: 3.3 g
- Protein: 5.5 g
- Carbohydrates: 32.9 g
- Fiber: 19.4 g

120. Super Tasty Onion Petals

Preparation time: 10 minutes

Cooking time: 15 minutes

Servings: 4

Ingredients:

- 13 oz onion, peeled
- 1 tsp basil, dried
- 1 tsp ground coriander
- 1 tbsp olive oil
- 1/4 tsp ground nutmeg
- 3/4 tsp turmeric

Directions:

1. Cut the onion into the petals and sprinkle with the basil, ground coriander, olive oil, ground nutmeg, and turmeric.
2. Mix the onion petals and transfer them to the air fryer basket.
3. Cook the petals for 15 minutes at 375°F. Stir the petals every 3 minutes.
4. When the onion petals are cooked—they will have a soft texture.
5. Serve the side dish immediately!

Nutrition:

- Calories: 69
- Fat: 3.7 g
- Protein: 1 g
- Carbohydrates: 9 g
- Fiber: 2.1 g

121. Eggplant Garlic Salad With Tomatoes

Preparation time: 10 minutes

Cooking time: 15 minutes

Servings: 6

Ingredients:

- 3 tomatoes, chopped
- 2 eggplants, chopped
- 1 tbsp olive oil
- 1 tsp avocado oil
- 1 tbsp vinegar
- 1/2 tsp ground black pepper
- 1/2 tsp dried basil
- 2 garlic cloves, chopped

Directions:

1. Place the chopped eggplants in the air fryer.

2. Sprinkle the eggplants with olive oil, ground black pepper, and dried basil.
3. Stir the eggplants and cook for 15 minutes at 390°F. Stir the vegetables every 5 minutes.
4. Then place the tomatoes in the bowl.
5. Add cooked eggplants, vinegar, and chopped garlic.
6. Then sprinkle the salad with the avocado oil and stir it.
7. Serve the cooked salad or keep it in the fridge!

Nutrition:

- Calories: 80
- Fat: 2.9 g
- Protein: 2.4 g
- Carbohydrates: 13.6 g
- Fiber: 7.3 g

122. Curry Eggplants

Preparation time: 10 minutes

Cooking time: 14 minutes

Servings: 2

Ingredients:

- 2 eggplants
- 1 tsp vinegar
- 1 tbsp olive oil
- 1 tsp curry powder
- 1 garlic clove
- 3 tbsp chicken stock

Directions:

1. Peel the eggplants and cut them into cubes.
2. Sprinkle the eggplants with the curry powder and chicken stock.
3. Put the vegetables in the air fryer and cook for 14 minutes at 390°F.
4. Stir the eggplants every 5 minutes.
5. When the eggplants are cooked—let them chill till the room temperature.
6. Sprinkle the vegetables with olive oil and vinegar. Stir and serve!

Nutrition:

- Calories: 204
- Fat: 8.2 g
- Protein: 5.7 g
- Carbohydrates: 33.4 g
- Fiber: 19.7 g

123. Sauteed Asparagus

Preparation time: 10 minutes

Cooking time: 8 minutes

Servings: 2

Ingredients:

- 1 onion, chopped
- 1/2 lemon
- 14 oz asparagus
- 1 tsp ghee
- 1 tsp salt

Directions:

1. Place the onion, salt, and ghee in the air fryer basket.
2. Cook it at 400°F for 2 minutes.
3. Meanwhile, chop the asparagus roughly.
4. Place the chopped asparagus in the air fryer basket.
5. Squeeze the lemon juice over the asparagus and stir it.
6. Cook the side dish for 6 minutes at 395°F. Stir it every 3 minutes of cooking.
7. Let the cooked asparagus chill a little. Enjoy!

Nutrition:

- Calories: 86
- Fat: 2.5 g
- Protein: 5.2 g
- Carbohydrates: 14.8 g
- Fiber: 5.9 g

124. Roasted Apple With Bacon

Preparation time: 20 minutes

Cooking time: 10 minutes

Servings: 8

Ingredients:

- 6 apples
- 7 oz bacon, chopped
- 1/2 tsp salt
- 1/2 tsp paprika
- 1/2 tsp ground black pepper
- 1 tbsp avocado oil

Directions:

1. Make medium holes in the apples.
2. Combine together the chopped bacon, salt, paprika, ground black pepper, and avocado oil.
3. Stir the mixture.
4. Fill the apple holes with the bacon mixture.
5. Put the apples in the air fryer basket.
6. Cook the apples for 10 minutes at 380°F.
7. When the time is over and the apples are cooked—chill them for 6 minutes and serve!

Nutrition:

- Calories: 224
- Fat: 10.9 g
- Protein: 9.7 g
- Carbohydrates: 23.7
- Fiber: 4.2 g

125. Fennel Slices

Preparation time: 10 minutes

Cooking time: 10 minutes

Servings: 2

Ingredients:

- 12 oz fennel bulb
- 1 tsp paprika
- 1/2 tsp chili flakes
- 1 tbsp olive oil
- 1 tsp cilantro, dried

Directions:

1. Slice the fennel bulb and sprinkle it with the paprika, chili flakes, and dried cilantro on each side.
2. Then sprinkle the fennel with the olive oil and transfer the vegetables to the air fryer basket.
3. Cook the fennel slices for 10 minutes at 380°F. Flip the fennel slices into another side after 5 minutes of cooking.
4. Enjoy the cooked side dish!

Nutrition:

- Calories: 116
- Fat: 7.5 g
- Protein: 2.3 g
- Carbohydrates: 13 g
- Fiber: 5.7 g

126. Butternut Squash Rice

Preparation time: 10 minutes

Cooking time: 20 minutes

Servings: 4

Ingredients:

- 1 lb. butternut squash
- 1 tbsp ghee
- 1 onion, diced
- 1 tsp salt
- 1 oz fresh parsley, chopped
- 1 tbsp olive oil

Directions:

1. Chop the butternut squash into the rice pieces.
2. Put the ghee in the air fryer basket and add diced onion.
3. Sprinkle the onion with salt and olive oil.
4. Cook it at 400°F for 2 minutes.
5. Then stir the onion and add the butternut squash rice.
6. Stir it and cook the meal for 18 minutes at 380°F.
7. Stir the squash every 4 minutes.
8. When the meal is cooked—sprinkle it with the chopped parsley and stir.
9. Serve it immediately!

Nutrition:

- Calories: 123
- Fat: 6.9 g
- Protein: 1.7 g
- Carbohydrates: 16.3 g
- Fiber: 3.1 g

127. Eggplant Lasagna

Preparation time: 20 minutes

Cooking time: 30 minutes

Servings: 3

Ingredients:

- 1 eggplant
- 2 tomatoes
- 1 tbsp olive oil
- 1 onion, diced
- 1 garlic clove, chopped
- 1 tsp dried basil
- 1 tsp ground black pepper
- 1/2 tsp turmeric
- 1 tsp cumin
- 1/2 cup chicken stock
- 1 tbsp fresh dill, chopped
- 4 oz mushrooms, chopped

Directions:

1. Slice the eggplants.
2. Slice the tomatoes.
3. Combine together the diced onion, olive oil, chopped garlic, dried basil, ground black pepper, turmeric, cumin, and fresh dill in the bowl.
4. Stir the mixture.
5. Then make the layer of the sliced eggplants in the air fryer basket.
6. Sprinkle it with the spice mixture.
7. Put the tomatoes over the eggplants and add mushrooms.
8. Sprinkle the vegetables with the spice mixture and repeat all the steps till you finish all the ingredients.
9. Add chicken stock and cook lasagna for 30 minutes at 365°F.
10. Let the cooked lasagna chill a little and serve it!

Nutrition:

- Calories: 127
- Fat: 5.6 g
- Protein: 4.4 g
- Carbohydrates: 18.9 g
- Fiber: 8 g

128. Stuffed Eggplants With Cherry Tomatoes

Preparation time: 15 minutes

Cooking time: 25 minutes

Servings: 2

Ingredients:

- 1 eggplant
- 5 oz cherry tomatoes
- 1 shallot, chopped
- 1/2 tsp salt
- 3/4 tsp nutmeg
- 3/4 tsp chili pepper
- 1 tbsp olive oil

Directions:

1. Cut the eggplant into halves.
2. Remove the meat from the eggplants.
3. Chop the cherry tomatoes and combine them together with the salt, shallot, nutmeg, chili pepper, and olive oil.
4. Stir the mixture.
5. Fill the eggplants with vegetables.
6. Put the stuffed vegetables in the air fryer basket and cook for 25 minutes at 370°F.
7. Then chill the cooked eggplants a little. Serve!

Nutrition:

- Calories: 136
- Fat: 7.9 g
- Protein: 3 g
- Carbohydrates: 16.9 g
- Fiber: 9.2 g

Chapter 14. Salads

129. Satisfying Spring Salad

Preparation time: 5 minutes

Cooking time: 10 minutes

Servings: 2

Ingredients:

- 4 oz arugula
- 1/2 cup cherry tomatoes halved
- 1/4 cup basil leaves
- 1/2 key lime, juiced

- 2 tbsp walnuts

Extra:

- 1/4 tsp salt
- 1/8 tsp cayenne pepper
- 1/2 tbsp tahini butter

Directions:

1. Prepare the dressing and for this, take a small bowl, place key lime juice in it, add tahini butter, salt, and cayenne pepper and then whisk until combined.
2. Take a medium bowl, place arugula, tomatoes, and basil leaves in it, pour in the dressing and then massage using your hands.
3. Let the salad rest for 20 minutes, then taste to adjust seasoning, and then serve with walnuts.

Nutrition:

- Calories: 87.
- Fat: 3.7 g
- Protein: 1.4 g
- Carbohydrates: 6.1 g
- Fiber: 1.3 g

130. The Raw Green Detox Salad

Preparation time: 5 minutes

Cooking time: 0 minutes

Servings: 2

Ingredients:

- 1/2 of cucumber, deseeded
- 4 oz arugula
- 1/8 tsp salt
- 1 tbsp key lime juice
- 1 tbsp olive oil

Extra:

- 1/8 tsp cayenne pepper

Directions:

1. Cut the cucumber into slices, add to a salad bowl, and then add arugula to it.

2. Mix lime juice and oil until combined, pour over the salad, and then season with salt and cayenne pepper.
3. Toss until mixed and then serve.

Nutrition:

- Calories: 142
- Fat: 12.5 g
- Protein: 1.6 g
- Carbohydrates: 7.8 g
- Fiber: 1.8 g

131. Dandelion Salad

Preparation time: 10 minutes

Cooking time: 7 minutes

Servings: 2

Ingredients:

- 1/2 of onion, peeled, sliced
- 5 strawberries, sliced
- 2 cups dandelion greens, rinsed
- 1 tbsp key lime juice
- 1 tbsp grapeseed oil

Extra:

- 1/4 tsp salt

Directions:

1. Take a medium skillet pan, place it over medium heat, add oil, and let it heat until warm.
2. Add onion, season with 1/8 tsp salt, stir until mixed, and then cook for 3 to 5 minutes until tender and golden brown.
3. Meanwhile, take a small bowl, place slices of strawberries in it, drizzle with 1/2 tbsp lime juice and then toss until coated.
4. When onions have turned golden brown, stir in remaining lime juice, stir until mixed, and then cook for 1 minute.
5. Remove pan from heat, transfer onions into a large salad bowl, add strawberries and juices, and dandelion greens, and then sprinkle with the remaining salt. Toss until mixed and then serve.

Nutrition:

- Calories: 204
- Fat: 16.1 g
- Protein: 7 g
- Carbohydrates: 10.6 g
- Fiber: 2.8 g

132. Spicy Wakame Salad

Preparation time: 15 minutes

Cooking time: 0 minutes

Servings: 2

Ingredients:

- 1 cup wakame stems
- 1/2 tbsp chopped red bell pepper
- 1/2 tsp onion powder
- 1/2 tbsp key lime juice

Extra:

- 1/2 tbsp agave syrup
- 1/2 tbsp sesame seeds
- 1/2 tbsp sesame oil

Directions:

1. Place wakame stems in a bowl, cover with water, let them soak for 10 minutes, and then drain.
2. Meanwhile, prepare the dressing and for this, take a small bowl, add lime juice, onion, agave syrup, and sesame oil in it and then whisk until blended.
3. Place drained wakame stems in a large dish, add bell pepper, pour in the dressing, and then toss until coated.
4. Sprinkle sesame seeds over the salad and then serve.

Nutrition:

- Calories: 106

- Fat: 7.3 g
- Protein: 3 g
- Carbohydrates: 8 g
- Fiber: 1.7 g

133. Avo-Orange Salad Dish

Preparation time: 5 minutes

Cooking time: 0 minutes

Servings: 2

Ingredients:

- 1 orange, peeled, sliced
- 4 cups greens
- 1/2 of avocado, peeled, pitted, diced
- 2 tbsp slivered red onion
- 1/2 cup cilantro

Extra:

- 1/4 tsp salt
- 1/4 cup olive oil
- 2 tbsp lime juice
- 2 tbsp orange juice

Directions:

1. Prepare the dressing and for this, place cilantro in a food processor, pour in orange juice, lime juice, and oil, add salt and then pulse until blended.
2. Tip the dressing into a mason jar. Add remaining ingredients, toss until coated, add to a salad bowl, or serve in the jar.

Nutrition:

- Calories: 106
- Fat: 7.3 g
- Protein: 3 g
- Carbohydrates: 8 g
- Fiber: 1.7 g

134. Nourishing Electric Salad

Preparation time: 5 minutes

Cooking time: 0 minutes

Servings: 2

Ingredients:

- 1/2 medium cucumber, deseeded, chopped
- 6 leaves of lettuce, broken into pieces
- 4 mushrooms, chopped
- 6 cherry tomatoes, chopped
- 10 olives

Extra:

- 1/2 of lime, juiced
- 1 tsp olive oil
- 1/4 tsp salt

Directions:

1. Take a medium salad bowl, place all the ingredients in it, and then toss until mixed.

Nutrition:

- Calories: 129
- Fat: 7 g
- Protein: 2 g
- Carbohydrates: 14 g
- Fiber: 4 g

135. Superfood Fonio Salad

Preparation time: 10 minutes

Cooking time: 5 minutes

Servings: 2

Ingredients:

- 1/2 cup cooked chickpeas
- 1/4 cup chopped cucumber
- 1/2 cup chopped red pepper
- 1/2 cup cherry tomatoes halved
- 1/2 cup fonio

Extra:

- 1/3 tsp salt
- 1 tbsp grapeseed oil
- 1/8 tsp cayenne pepper
- 1 key lime, juiced
- 1 cup spring water

Directions:

1. Take a medium saucepan, place it over high heat, pour in water, and bring it to a boil.
2. Add fonio, switch heat to the low level, cook for 1 minute, and then remove the pan from heat.
3. Cover the pan with its lid, let fonio rest for 5 minutes, fluff by using a fork, and then let it cool for 15 minutes.
4. Take a salad bowl, place lime juice and oil in it, and then stir in salt and cayenne pepper until combined.
5. Add remaining ingredients including fonio, toss until mixed, and then serve.

Nutrition:

- Calories: 145
- Fat: 3 g
- Protein: 6 g
- Carbohydrates: 24.5 g
- Fiber: 5.5 g

136. Healthy Chickpea Roast Salad

Preparation time: 10 minutes

Cooking time: 20 minutes

Servings: 2

Ingredients:

- 1/2 of cucumber, deseeded, sliced
- 2 avocados, peeled, pitted, cubed
- 1 medium white onion, peeled, diced
- 2 cups cooked chickpeas
- 1/4 cup chopped coriander

Extra:

- 1 tsp onion powder
- 1/2 tsp cayenne pepper
- 1 tsp sea salt
- 2 tbsp hemp seeds, shelled
- 1 key lime, juiced
- 1 tbsp olive oil

Directions:

1. Switch on the oven, then set it to 425°F and let it preheat.
2. Meanwhile, take a baking sheet, place chickpeas on it, season with salt, onion powder, and pepper, drizzle with oil and then toss until combined.
3. Bake the chickpeas for 20 minutes or until golden brown and crisp, then let them cool for 10 minutes.
4. Transfer chickpeas to a bowl, add the remaining ingredients and stir until combined.

Nutrition:

- Calories: 208.3
- Fat: 8 g
- Protein: 6.4 g
- Carbohydrates: 30 g
- Fiber: 8 g

137. Amaranth Tabbouleh Salad

Preparation time: 5 minutes

Cooking time: 10 minutes

Servings: 2

Ingredients:

- 1 small white onion, peeled, chopped
- 1 cup cooked amaranth
- 1/2 of cucumber, deseeded, chopped
- 1 cup cooked chickpeas
- 1/2 of medium red bell pepper, chopped

Extra:

- 1/3 tsp sea salt
- 1/8 tsp cayenne pepper
- 2 tbsp key lime juice

Directions:

1. Take a small bowl, place lime juice in it, add salt and stir until combined.
2. Place remaining ingredients in a salad bowl, drizzle with lime juice mixture, toss until mixed, and then serve.

Nutrition:

- Calories: 214
- Fat: 4.5 g
- Protein: 6.5 g
- Carbohydrates: 37 g
- Fiber: 9 g

138. Zucchini and Mushroom Bowl

Preparation time: 5 minutes

Cooking time: 8 minutes

Servings: 2

Ingredients:

- 2 zucchini, spiralized
- 1/2 of medium red bell pepper, sliced
- 1/2 cup sliced mushrooms
- 1/2 of medium green bell pepper, sliced
- 1/2 of medium white onion, peeled, sliced

Extra:

- 1/3 tsp salt
- 1/8 tsp cayenne pepper
- 1 tbsp grapeseed oil

Directions:

1. Take a large skillet pan, place it over medium-high heat, add oil, and when hot, add onion, mushrooms, and bell peppers, and then cook for 3 to 5 minutes until tender-crisp.
2. Add zucchini noodles, toss until mixed, and then cook for 2 minutes until warm.

Nutrition:

- Calories: 168
- Fat: 2 g
- Protein: 0.9 g
- Carbohydrates: 36 g
- Fiber: 6 g

139. Pear and Strawberry Salad

Preparation time: 15 minutes

Cooking time: 0 minutes

Servings: 4

Ingredients:

- 4 cups romaine lettuce, torn
- 2 pears, cored and sliced
- 1 cup fresh strawberries, hulled and sliced
- 1/4 cup walnuts, chopped
- 3 tbsp olive oil
- 2 tbsp fresh key lime juice
- 1 tbsp agave nectar

Directions:

1. In a salad bowl, place all ingredients and toss to coat well.
2. Serve immediately.

Nutrition:

- Calories: 8
- Fat: 1.8 g
- Protein: 2.8 g
- Carbohydrates: 25.2 g
- Fiber: 5.1 g
- Cholesterol: 0 mg

140. Raspberry and Arugula Salad

Preparation time: 15 minutes

Cooking time: 0 minutes

Servings: 2

Ingredients:

Salad:

- 3 cups fresh baby arugula

- 1 cup fresh raspberries
- 1/4 cup walnuts, chopped

Dressing:

- 1 tbsp olive oil
- 1 tbsp fresh key lime juice
- 1/2 tsp agave nectar
- Sea salt, as needed

Directions:

1. For the salad: Place all ingredients in a salad bowl and mix.
2. For the dressing: Place all ingredients in another bowl and beat until well combined.
3. Pour the dressing over the salad and toss to coat well. Serve immediately.

Nutrition:

- Calories: 202
- Fat: 1.6 g
- Protein: 5.3 g
- Carbohydrates: 11.4 g
- Fiber: 5.6 g
- Cholesterol: 0 mg

141. Mixed Berries Salad

Preparation time: 15 minutes

Cooking time: 15 minutes

Servings: 4

Ingredients:

- 1 cup fresh strawberries, hulled and sliced
- 1/2 cup fresh blackberries
- 1/2 cup fresh blueberries
- 1/2 cup fresh raspberries
- 6 cups fresh arugula
- 2 tbsp olive oil
- Sea salt, as needed

Directions:

1. In a salad bowl, place all Ingredients: and toss to coat well. Serve immediately.

Nutrition:

- Calories: 105
- Fat: 1 g
- Protein: 1.6 g
- Carbohydrates: 10.1 g
- Fiber: 3.6 g
- Cholesterol: 0 mg

142. Apple and Kale Salad

Preparation time: 15 minutes

Cooking time: 15 minutes

Servings: 4

Ingredients:

- 3 large apples, cored and sliced
- 6 cups fresh baby kale
- 1/4 cup walnuts, chopped
- 2 tbsp olive oil
- 1 tbsp agave nectar
- Sea salt, as needed

Directions:

1. In a salad bowl, place all ingredients and toss to coat well. Serve immediately.

Nutrition:

- Calories: 260
- Fat: 1.3 g
- Protein: 5.3 g
- Carbohydrates: 38.4 g
- Fiber: 6.3 g
- Cholesterol: 0 mg

143. Mango and Arugula Salad

Preparation time: 15 minutes

Cooking time: 15 minutes

Servings: 6

Ingredients:

- 2 1/2 cups mangoes; peeled, pitted, and sliced
- 2 1/2 cups avocados; peeled, pitted, and sliced
- 1 red onion, sliced
- 6 cups fresh baby arugula
- 1/4 cup fresh mint leaves, chopped
- 2 tbsp fresh orange juice
- Sea salt, as needed

Directions:

1. Place all ingredients in a salad bowl and gently toss to combine.
2. Cover and refrigerate to chill before serving.

Nutrition:

- Calories: 182
- Fat: 2.6 g
- Protein: 2.6 g
- Carbohydrates: 18.8 g
- Fiber: 6.2 g
- Cholesterol: 0 mg

144. Orange and Kale Salad

Preparation time: 10 minutes

Cooking time: 10 minutes

Servings: 2

Ingredients:

Salad:

- 3 cups fresh kale, tough ribs removed and torn
- 2 oranges, peeled and segmented
- 2 tbsp fresh cranberries

Dressing:

- 2 tbsp olive oil
- 2 tbsp fresh orange juice
- 1/2 tsp agave nectar
- Sea salt, as needed

Directions:

1. For the salad: Place all ingredients in a salad bowl and mix.
2. For the dressing: Place all ingredients in n another bowl and beat until well combined.
3. Pour the dressing over the salad and toss to coat well. Serve immediately.

Nutrition:

- Calories: 272
- Fat: 2 g
- Protein: 4.8 g
- Carbohydrates: 35.7 g
- Fiber: 6.3 g
- Cholesterol: 0 mg

145. Zucchini and Tomato Salad

Preparation time: 15 minutes

Cooking time: 15 minutes

Servings: 4

Ingredients:

- 2 medium zucchinis, sliced thinly
- 2 cups plum tomatoes, sliced
- 2 tbsp olive oil
- 2 tbsp fresh key lime juice
- A pinch of sea salt

Directions:

1. In a salad bowl, place all ingredients and gently toss to combine. Serve immediately.

Nutrition:

- Calories: 93
- Fat: 1.1 g
- Protein: 2 g
- Carbohydrates: 6.9 g
- Fiber: 2.2 g
- Cholesterol: 0 mg

146. Tomato and Arugula Salad

Preparation time: 15 minutes

Cooking time: 15 minutes

Servings: 4

Ingredients:

- 6 cups fresh baby arugula
- 2 cups cherry tomatoes
- 2 scallions, chopped
- 2 tbsp olive oil
- 2 tbsp fresh orange juice
- Sea salt, as needed

Directions:

1. In a salad bowl, place all ingredients and toss to combine.
2. Cover the bowl and refrigerate for about 6 to 8 hours.
3. Remove from the refrigerator and toss well before serving.

Nutrition:

- Calories: 90
- Fat: 1.1 g
- Protein: 1.8 g
- Carbohydrates: 6 g
- Fiber: 1.8 g
- Cholesterol: 0 mg

147. Warm Avo and Quinoa Salad

Preparation time: 5 minutes

Cooking time: 12 minutes

Servings: 4

Ingredients:

- 4 ripe avocados, quartered
- 1 cup quinoa
- 4/5 lb Chickpeas, drained
- 1 oz flat-leaf parsley
- 2 cups water
- Salt and pepper to taste

Directions:

1. Add quinoa to a pot with 2 cups water. Bring to a boil then simmer for 12 minutes or until all the water has evaporated. The grains should be glassy and swollen.
2. Toss the quinoa with all other ingredients and season with salt and pepper to taste.
3. Serve with olive oil and lemon wedges. Enjoy.

Nutrition:

- Calories: 354
- Fat: 16 g
- Protein: 15 g
- Carbohydrates: 31 g
- Fiber: 15 g

148. Chickpeas and Quinoa Salad

Preparation time: 20 minutes

Cooking time: 20 minutes

Servings: 8

Ingredients:

- 1 3/4 cups spring water
- 1 cup quinoa, rinsed
- Sea salt, as needed
- 2 cups cooked chickpeas
- 1 medium red bell pepper, seeded and chopped
- 1 medium green bell pepper, seeded and chopped
- 2 large cucumbers, chopped
- 1/2 cup onion, chopped
- 3 tbsp olive oil
- 4 tbsp fresh basil leaves, chopped

Directions:

1. In a pan, add the water over high heat and bring it to a boil.
2. Add the quinoa and salt and cook until boiling.
3. Now, adjust the heat to low and simmer, covered for about 15 to 20 minutes or until all the liquid is absorbed.
4. Remove from the heat and set aside, covered for about 5 to 10 minutes.
5. Uncover and with a fork, fluff the quinoa.

6. In a salad bowl, place quinoa with the remaining ingredients and gently toss to coat. Serve immediately.

Nutrition:

- Calories: 215
- Fat: 1 g
- Protein: 7.5 g
- Carbohydrates: 30.5 g
- Fiber: 5.6 g
- Cholesterol: 0 mg

149. Quinoa, Tomato, and Mango Salad

Preparation time: 15 minutes

Cooking time: 0 minutes

Servings: 4

Ingredients:

- 2 cups mango; peeled, pitted, and chopped
- 1 cup cooked quinoa
- 1 green bell pepper, seeded and chopped
- 1 cup cherry tomato, halved
- 1/2 cup fresh parsley, chopped
- 1/4 cup onion, sliced
- 2 garlic cloves, minced
- 2 tbsp fresh key lime juice
- 1 1/2 tbsp olive oil
- A pinch of sea salt

Directions:

1. In a salad bowl, place all ingredients and gently stir to combine.
2. Refrigerate for about 1 to 2 hours before serving.

Nutrition:

- Calories: 270
- Fat: 1.2 g
- Protein: 7.8 g
- Carbohydrates: 45.3 g
- Fiber: 5.7 g
- Cholesterol: 0 mg

Chapter 15. Snacks

150. Falafel

Preparation time: 10 minutes

Cooking time: 10 minutes

Servings: 2

Ingredients:

- 2 cups cooked chickpeas
- 1/2 cup chopped white onion
- 1/2 cup chickpea flour
- 1/4 cup green onions, chopped
- 1 tsp chopped basil

Extra:

- 1 tsp chopped oregano
- 1 tsp onion powder
- 1/2 tsp sea salt
- 1/2 tsp cayenne pepper
- 1/3 cup water from cooked chickpeas
- 1 tbsp lime juice
- 1 tbsp tahini
- 1 tbsp grapeseed oil

Directions:

1. Add chickpeas into a food processor, add remaining ingredients except for oil and then pulse until well blended.
2. Tip the mixture into a bowl and then shape into even size patties.
3. Take a large skillet pan, place it over medium heat, add oil and when hot, place prepared falafel patties in it and then cook for 4 to 5 minutes per side until golden brown and cooked.

Nutrition:

- Calories: 182
- Fat: 10 g
- Protein: 6 g
- Carbohydrates: 18 g
- Fiber: 4 g

151. Sloppy Joe

Preparation time: 5 minutes

Cooking time: 12 minutes

Servings: 2

Ingredients:

- 1/4 cup chopped white onion
- 1 cup cooked Kamut
- 1/4 cup chopped green bell pepper
- 1/2 cup cooked chickpeas
- 3/4 cup Barbecue Sauce, Alkaline

Extra:

- 1/2 tsp sea salt
- 1/8 tsp cayenne powder
- 1/2 tsp onion powder
- 1/2 tbsp grapeseed oil

Directions:

1. Place chickpeas and Kamut in a food processor and then pulse until combined.
2. Then take a large skillet pan, place it over medium-high heat, add oil, and when hot, add

onion and peppers into the pan, stir in all the seasonings and then cook for 5 minutes until tender.
3. Add blended chickpea mixture, add remaining ingredients, stir until mixed, and then simmer it for 5 minutes.

Nutrition:

- Calories: 166.5
- Fat: 2.5 g
- Protein: 7 g
- Carbohydrates: 32.5 g
- Fiber: 6 g

152. Sausage Links

Preparation time: 10 minutes

Cooking time: 10 minutes

Servings: 2

Ingredients:

- 1 cup cooked chickpeas
- 2 cherry tomatoes
- 1/2 cup sliced mushrooms
- 1/4 cup chopped white onion
- 1/4 cup chickpea flour

Extra:

- 1/2 tsp basil
- 1/2 tsp oregano
- 1/2 tsp sea salt
- 1/2 tsp cayenne powder
- 1/2 tsp dill
- 1 tbsp grapeseed oil

Directions:

1. Place all the ingredients in a food processor except for chickpeas and then pulse until combined.
2. Add chickpeas, blend again until well combined, and then spoon the mixture into a piping bag.
3. Take a large skillet pan, place it over medium-high heat, add oil and then hot, squeeze chickpea mixture to make sausage links, and then cook for 3 to 4 minutes per side until nicely brown and cooked.

Nutrition:

- Calories: 187.1
- Fat: 7.4 g
- Protein: 7.3 g
- Carbohydrates: 24.2 g
- Fiber: 6.3 g

153. Chickpea Nuggets

Preparation time: 10 minutes

Cooking time: 30 minutes

Servings: 2

Ingredients:

- 2 cups cooked chickpeas
- 1/2 tsp salt
- 1 tsp onion powder
- 1/3 cup and 1 tbsp bread crumbs
- Olive oil to taste

Directions:

1. Switch on the oven, then set it to 350°F and let it preheat.
2. Meanwhile, place chickpeas in a food processor and then pulse until crumbled.
3. Tip the chickpeas into a bowl, add the remaining ingredients in it except for 1/3 cup of breadcrumbs, and then stir until a chunky mixture comes together.
4. Shape the mixture into evenly sized balls, shape each ball into a nugget, arrange on a baking sheet greased with oil and then bake for 15 minutes per side until golden brown.

Nutrition:

- Calories: 291.6
- Fat: 3.9 g
- Protein: 19.9 g
- Carbohydrates: 26.8 g
- Fiber: 3.4 g

Chapter 16. 28-Day Meal Plan

Below you will find an example of a meal plan to get you started right away. However, by combining all the recipes in the book, you can create a 1900-day meal plan.

Days	Breakfast	Lunch	Dinner	Snacks
1	Liver detox smoothie	Mixed veggies and grapefruit salad with Dijon grapefruit vinaigrette	Delicious raw bean salad	Falafel
2	High-protein French toast	Quick hummus and Greek salad	Chicken and farro herb salad	Sloppy joe
3	Broccoli salad	Quick pesto chicken salad with greens	Yummy cedar planked salmon	Sausage links
4	Classic eggs benedict with lemon basil hollandaise	Crispy tofu with vegetable salad	Quick delicious maple salmon	Chickpea nuggets
5	Blueberry smoothie	Healthy spinach salad	Bruschetta chicken stuffed avocados	Chickpea flour quiche
6	Fried egg and greens	Roasted chicken and mushrooms salad	Baked Dijon salmon	Vegan veggie fritters
7	Sweet potato pie smoothie bowl	Chickpea, broccoli, and pomegranate salad	Pan seared salmon	Pesto zoodles
8	cornmeal pancakes with black bean salsa & cilantro yogurt	anchovy, orange and olive salad	blackened salmon fillets	peach muffin
9	Southwestern-style black bean burritos	Vegetable and chickpea salad	Balsamic-glazed salmon fillets	Energy balls
10	Fruit yogurt parfait	Tabouli with veggies salad	Alaska salmon bake with pecan crunch coating	Quinoa bowl
11	Peanut butter maple banana muffins	Healthy Fattoush salad	Lemon rosemary salmon	Spelt and raisin cookies
12	Ultimate liver detox soup	Veggies with chickpea salad	Chocolate covered grapefruit	Salad burritos
13	Pineapple, matcha, and beet chia pudding	Couscous with artichokes, sun-dried tomatoes and feta	Salmon turmeric soup recipe	Chickpea and quinoa burgers
14	Chicken souvlaki	Lemon muffins	Quinoa cucumber salad	Peach and walnuts smoothie
15	Overnight superfood parfait	Citrus chicken with delicious cold soup	Broccoli, quinoa, and chicken salad	Mushroom gravy
16	Onion omelet	Eggs and veggies	Vegetable and white bean salad	Spring salad

17	Stuffed figs	Toxin flush and detox salad	Quinoa chicken salad	Tamarind cucumber breakfast drink
18	Superfood liver cleansing soup	Olive and milk bread	Olive, watermelon, feta &caper salad	Raspberries energy balls
19	Asparagus with egg	Mixed veggies and grapefruit salad with Dijon grapefruit vinaigrette	Spiralized crisp cucumber salad	Nori burritos
20	Vanilla oats	Quick hummus and Greek salad	Delicious raw bean salad	Kale pesto pasta
21	Carrot omelet	Quick pesto chicken salad with greens	Chicken and farro herb salad	Falafel
22	Veggie omelet	Crispy tofu with vegetable salad	Yummy cedar planked salmon	Sloppy joe
23	Beets omelet	Healthy spinach salad	Quick delicious maple salmon	Sausage links
24	Spiced French toast	Roasted chicken and mushrooms salad	Bruschetta chicken stuffed avocados	Chickpea nuggets
25	Liver detox smoothie	Chickpea, broccoli, and pomegranate salad	Baked Dijon salmon	Chickpea flour quiche
26	High protein French toast	Anchovy, orange, and olive salad	Pan seared salmon	Vegan veggie fritters
27	Broccoli salad	Vegetable and chickpea salad	Blackened salmon fillets	Pesto zoodles
28	Classic eggs benedict with lemon basil hollandaise	Tabouli with veggies salad	Balsamic-glazed salmon fillets	Peach muffin

Conclusion

Having a liver disease is not a death sentence, and it may be treated to the point that you can enjoy all parts of your life. The first signs of a failing liver include foul breath, bloating, heartburn, sudden weight loss, and premature graying of the hair. Countless fatty liver sufferers show no symptoms or negative effects until too late. You need to be more vigilant and adjust your diet and lifestyle. The recipes in this cookbook can help you avoid developing a fatty liver. In general, we should examine how the liver and the rest of the body are affected by fatty liver. Proactiveness is essential. If you decided to wait until the last minute, you may miss out on opportunities. Be mindful of your liver's capacity. The best way you can get started is to take it one step at a time. Follow the recipes in this book, and you'll be on your way to a healthy liver in no time. I hope your health continues to improve in the years to come. As a result of this procedure, you will feel rejuvenated.

Of course, not everyone will be receptive to the method. Still, none of the ingredients used are dangerous in any way, and the results speak for themselves.

This book has explained everything you can do to take away accumulated fat in your liver as well as remove harmful deposits in it such as gallbladder stones. This is information you should know so that you would be able to determine if you are suffering from this condition. If you know what you are experiencing, you can prevent the disease from worsening.

Excessive calories can make fat build-up in your liver and the latter will then have a hard time performing its function which is to break fats down. Overconsumption of alcohol can also make fat accumulate in your liver. Genetics is also a possible cause.

If you fail to treat liver diseases such as fatty liver, this organ will become scarred and hardened and you will suffer from a serious condition called cirrhosis. Eventually, cirrhosis will result in liver failure. This condition has a few symptoms so you may not see signs of having it.

The Liver Cleanse is a way of decongesting your liver, the bile ducts that are critical to its functions, and your colon immediately. With a process that only lasts from the evening of one day to the morning of the next, you can get rid of the gallstones obstructing your system. And yes, you still get your regular eight-hour sleep.

Ingredients introduced to the system during the flush will soften and break down the gallstones. They'll dilate and oil the bile ducts to ensure the now softened gallstones travel through the body with as little drama as possible. It is an easy, pain-free, and safe process that will leave you feeling like a new person.

The effects of the Liver Cleanse are almost immediate. You will feel the immediate rejuvenation of your system. Your digestive system will be cleaned out. Your blood will be purified. The hormones in your body will be balanced better and your cells will be able to regenerate faster. You will look, feel and be better!

Everyone should do a Liver Cleanse at least once in their lifetime if not more. The benefits that come with it are incredible. Think of your body as a car that requires frequent servicing to increase its capacity to perform. Like servicing, the Liver Cleanse will energize and revitalize you and ultimately increase your life expectancy. If you follow the instructions for both the preparation week and the overnight flush, precisely as prescribed, you'll be well on your way to better health.

Of course, not everyone will be open-minded to the process but none of the ingredients used are in any way harmful and the results afterward speak for themselves.

Thank you for getting this far. I have put a lot of time and effort and dedication into writing this book. Now I kindly ask you to help me; I would be very, very pleased to receive your positive review on Amazon; reviews are much more important than you imagine!

Index

A

Amaranth Tabbouleh Salad

Anchovy, Orange, and Olive Salad

Apple and Kale Salad

Apple Pie Smoothie

Apple, Quinoa, and Fig Smoothie

Arugula and Sweet Potato Salad

Asparagus With Egg

Avo-Orange Salad Dish

B

Balsamic Radishes

Banana Herbal Drink

Banana Sea Moss Smoothie

Beef Meatballs

Beef Stovies

Beef Tripe Pot

Beets Omelet

Black COD

BlackBerry and Banana Smoothie

Blueberry Smoothie

Bok Choy and Sprouts

Brisket and Ale Pot Roast

Broccoli Salad

Butternut Squash Rice

Buttery Cod

C

Cantaloupe Smoothie Tea

Carrot Omelet

Carrots Sauté

Chamomile Delight Smoothie

Cheesy Scrambled Eggs With Fresh Herbs

Cherry Tomatoes Sauté

Chicken and Black Beans

Chicken and Butter Sauce

Chicken and Lemongrass Sauce

Chicken Souvlaki

Chickpea Nuggets

Chickpea, Broccoli, and Pomegranate Salad

Chickpeas and Quinoa Salad

Chinese Bok Choy and Turkey Soup

Cinnamon Baby Carrot

Citrus Chicken With Delicious Cold Soup

Classic Eggs Benedict With Lemon Basil Hollandaise

Cornmeal Pancakes With Black Bean Salsa and Cilantro Yogurt

Couscous With Artichokes, Sun-Dried Tomatoes, and Feta

Crab Legs

Creamy Eggplant

Crispy Fish

Crispy Tofu With Vegetable Salad

Crusty Pesto Salmon

Curry Eggplants

D

Dandelion Salad

E

Easy Zucchini Beef Lasagna

Eggplant and Carrots Mix

Eggplant Garlic Salad With Tomatoes

Eggplant Lasagna

Eggplant Tongues

Eggs and Veggies

F

Falafel

Fennel Slices

Festive Turkey Rouladen

Foil Packet Salmon

Fried Egg and Greens

Fruit Yogurt Parfait

G

Green Sea Moss Drink

Green Smoothie With Raspberries

Green Smoothie

Green Tea and Lettuce Detox Smoothie

Grilled Sirloin Steak With Sauce Diane

H

Healthy Chickpea Roast Salad

Healthy Fattoush Salad

Healthy Spinach Salad

Herby Chicken Meatloaf

High Protein French Toast

Honey Dew and Arugula Smoothie

K

Kale Sauté

L

Lemon and Garlic Barbecued Ocean Trout With Green Salad

Lemon Garlic Shrimp

Lemon Muffins

Lettuce, Banana, and Berries Smoothie

Liver Detox Smoothie

Lovely Pulled Chicken Egg Bites

M

Mango and Arugula Salad

Miso-Glazed Salmon

Mixed Berries Salad

Mixed Veggies and Grapefruit Salad With Dijon Grapefruit Vinaigrette

Moules Marinieres

N

Nicoise Salad

Nourishing Electric Salad

O

Olive and Milk Bread

Onion Omelet

Orange and Kale Salad

Orange and Lettuce Smoothie

Overnight Superfood Parfait

P

Pan-Fried Chorizo Sausage

Parmesan Eggplants

Parsley Zucchini and Radishes

Peanut Butter Maple Banana Muffins

Pear and Strawberry Salad

Pineapple, Matcha, and Beet Chia Pudding

Q

Quick Hummus and Greek Salad

Quick Pesto Chicken Salad With Greens

Quinoa, Tomato, and Mango Salad

R

Raspberry and Arugula Salad

Refreshing Smoothie With Nuts

Rib Roast With Roasted Shallots and Garlic

Roasted Apple With Bacon

Roasted Chicken and Mushrooms Salad

S

Sabich Sandwich

Saffron Beef

Salmon Burgers

Salmon Pasta

Salmon With Vegetables

Satisfying Spring Salad

Sausage Links

Sauteed Asparagus

Seared Scallops

Sesame Chicken With Black Rice, Broccoli, and Snap Peas

Sesame Tuna Steak

Shrimp Curry

Shrimp With Garlic

Sloppy Joe

Smoothie Bowl

Southwestern-Style Black Bean Burritos

Spaghetti Squash Casserole

Spiced French Toast

Spicy Wakame Salad

Steamed Mussels With Coconut-Curry

Strawberry Shake

Stuffed Eggplants With CherryTomatoes

Stuffed Figs

Super Tasty Onion Petals

Superfood Fonio Salad

Superfood Liver Cleansing Soup

Sweet Chipotle Grilled Beef Ribs

Sweet Green Drink

Sweet Potato Pie Smoothie Bowl

Sweet Sunrise Smoothie

T

Tabouli With Veggies Salad

Tasty Lamb Ribs

The Raw Green Detox Salad

Tomato and Arugula Salad

Toxin Flush and Detox Salad

Tuna Noodle Casserole

U

Ultimate Liver Detox Soup

V

Vanilla Oats

Vegetable and Chickpea Salad

Veggie Omelet

Veggie-Ful Smoothie

Veggies With Chickpea Salad

W

Warm Avo and Quinoa Salad

Watermelon and Strawberries Drink

Watermelon Juice

Watermelon, Cantaloupe, and Mango Smoothie

Z

Zucchini and Mushroom Bowl

Zucchini and Tomato Salad

Made in United States
North Haven, CT
07 August 2023